Angela Kuttner Botelho

German Jews and the Persistence of Jewish Identity in Conversion

Angela Kuttner Botelho

German Jews and the Persistence of Jewish Identity in Conversion

Writing the Jewish Self

DE GRUYTER
OLDENBOURG

ISBN 978-3-11-127075-3
e-ISBN (PDF) 978-3-11-073196-5
e-ISBN (EPUB) 978-3-11-073206-1

Library of Congress Control Number: 2021936923

Bibliographic information published by the Deutsche Nationalbibliothek
The Deutsche Nationalbibliothek lists this publication in the Deutsche Nationalbibliografie;
detailed bibliographic data are available on the Internet at http://dnb.dnb.de.

© 2023 Walter de Gruyter GmbH, Berlin/Boston
This volume is text- and page-identical with the hardback published in 2021.
Cover Image: Photograph by Francis Kuttner. Permission granted
Print and Binding: CPI books GmbH, Leck

www.degruyter.com

To my beloved daughter Abigail,
Who gave me new life,
And to my precious grandchildren Ava and June,
As you move into your future
May you treasure your family's past.

Acknowledgments

First and foremost, I wish to highlight the enormous, quite different contributions of two women who between them brought this project to fruition: Naomi Seidman and Julia Brauch. Without each of them this book would not have come into being.

To start at the beginning, it was Naomi Seidman who lured me into enrolling in the Master's program in Jewish History and Culture at the Richard S. Dinner Center for Jewish Studies at Berkeley's Graduate Theological Union in 2010. This was after I, a somewhat timid newbie auditor in her course on Modern Jewish History, spontaneously burst out amidst the Marrano segment, "Oh, I didn't know there were any other Jews in the world who had been baptized!" Naomi's response after class was an invitation to coffee; the rest is history. As my mentor and thesis advisor over the next three years, her never-failing support and sheer intellectual heft served to inspire and shape every aspect of my MA trajectory which in turn became the seed for the book project that consumed the next several years of my life. Currently the Chancellor Jackman Professor in the Arts at the University of Toronto, Naomi nonetheless expressed a wholehearted willingness to review my completed book manuscript long after I had ceased to be her actual student. As it turned out, her contribution became the decisive factor in De Gruyter's decision to commit to my work. To me, Naomi Seidman's efforts on my behalf are a testament to her enormous, all too rare generosity of spirit as well as to her deep commitment to an expansive view of Jewish history in which my own work, hopefully, will play its own small part. I am deeply grateful.

For her part, as Acquisitions Editor for Jewish Studies and History with De Gruyter Publishing, Julia Brauch's unstinting enthusiasm for my work dating from my very first contact with her, followed by her tireless efforts to shepherd my monograph through a rigorous internal review process, have led directly to the current happy and successful outcome. She has been a wonderful gift to me as well.

I also wish to acknowledge the contributions of Deena Aranoff, who specializes in Medieval Jewish History at the Graduate Theological Union's Center for Jewish Studies. Deena's deeply informed teaching, coupled with her unfailingly warm support, gave me the opportunity to recover the richness and depth of an immense premodern Jewish heritage that was totally new to me.

I also want to note the Graduate Theological Union's generosity in according me the status of Visiting Scholar over the last several post-graduate years, thus affording me ready access to its Florence Lamson Hewlett Library as well as to the University of California's immense research resources.

https://doi.org/10.1515/9783110731965-001

Finally, I owe a deep debt of gratitude to my friends. Proceeding by choice as an independent scholar in my post-MA phase (I wasn't sure if I had enough years left in me to submit to the rigors of a Ph.D. program and then embark on a book project), I relied on the indispensible support and encouragement of the friends I made during my graduate student years to see me through. I highlight in particular the contributions of Susan Aguilar and Sarah Cramsey. Both were consistently there for me, offering numerous stimulating and insightful comments on my various drafting dilemmas, making me laugh, and in general providing much needed intellectual companionship and personal support despite the demands of their own busy schedules as newly minted PhDs forging new careers. Other fellow students from my GTU days, Nicholas Baer and Shaina Hammerman, cheered me on from afar as they pursued their own career paths.

Reaching out more widely, I want to mention my friend Eva Lipman, who in the last years of the project unstintingly gifted me with her strong literary sensibilities as she critiqued various iterations of my manuscript. I also especially want to thank my friends Bernie and Roz Steinberg, who unfailingly and with great sensitivity supported my sometimes uncertain piecing together of a Jewish identity arising out of a contested Jewish background. Finally, I must further acknowledge my friend Paul Veres, jack of all trades, who transformed my often tattered family photos into a serviceable high resolution and worked with me to create for them a beautiful layout. I also need to mention my yoga community at the Berkeley Yoga Center and my many friends at Congregation Beth El, all of whom remained unfailingly supportive of my efforts whether or not they understood what I was doing. They were the stuff of my daily life, and are important to me.

Turning at last to my family, I remain grateful from the bottom of my heart to all my twenty-five interviewees, my brothers, sisters, daughter, nephews, and nieces. Their thoughts on their own idiosyncratic relationship to our shared Jewish heritage are at the core of this project, and I could not have done it without them. I count the memories of my experiences with each of them, my close relatives, suffused with the warmth and hospitality they unfailingly displayed, as among the most cherished of my life.

Special mention goes out to my brother Thomas Kuttner, my fellow traveler in this sometimes painful family reclamation project. His deep archival knowledge of our family's history, his immediate grasp of the importance of this project not only to our family but also to the Jewish community at large, his generous appraisals of my unfolding work product, informed by his own deep scholarship, have been an enormous benefit to me over the years.

Last, but by no means least, I owe a huge debt of gratitude to my husband, Barry Silverblatt. Without his unfailing support and encouragement, his willingness to serve as my roadie as we traversed the continent creating videotaped interviews of my far-flung relatives, his always available sharp-eyed proofreading, his absolutely irreplaceable computer knowledge coming to my rescue time and time again, his willingness to allow me to disappear for months on end into our study while he forged on alone with only ESPN for companionship, his rock-and-roll presence at the end of a long hard week, and above all, his dead-on sense of humor, I don't know if I could have finished this project. Thank you.

Family Cast of Characters

Stephan Kuttner (1907 – 1996)
Eva Kuttner (1914 – 2007)

Their Children
– Ludwig Kuttner (1934)
– Andrew Kuttner (1936 – 1969)
– Susanne Potts (1940)
– Angela Botelho (1942)
– Barbara DiConstanzo (1944)
– Thomas Kuttner (1946)
– Michael Kuttner (1948)
– Francis Kuttner (1951)
– Philip Kuttner (1953)

Ludwig's children
– Ann Kuttner (1957)
– Stephan Kuttner (1959)
– Nicholas Kuttner (1960)
– Elizabeth Kuttner (1961)
– Jessica Lefkow (1962)
– Anthony Kuttner (1964)

Andrew's Children
– Charles Kuttner (1962)
– Michele Kuttner (1963)
– Deborah Kuttner (1969)

Susanne's Children
– Martha Fishman (1962)
– John Potts (1963)
– Stephan Potts (1968)

Angela's Children
– Abigail Frank (1974)

Barbara's Children
– Lisa DiConstranzo (1976)
– Nicholas DiCostanzo (1980)

Thomas' Children
– Stephanie Kuttner (1972)
– Ben Kuttner (1975)
– David Kuttner (1980)

Limited to Direct Descendants of Stephan and Eva Kuttner.

https://doi.org/10.1515/9783110731965-002

Contents

Preface

Picture us, a large German Jewish refugee family become Catholic in the 1940s and early 1950s in Washington, D.C. Eventually there would be nine children, the first three born in Rome between 1934 and 1940 and the next six in America between 1942 (that would be me) and 1953. My father, a scholar, remote as I remember him, buried in his study, cigarettes and wine at hand. My mother, warm, emotive, singlehandedly managing her large household with a characteristic touch of iron. We children were a gang—high-spirited, close in age, intensely aware of one another and our relationships.

My mother often recounted to us our origin story. This is how I remember it.

Here is how we escaped the Nazis, my mother would begin. We lived in Rome in an apartment, your grandparents nearby. It was 1940. Nazis and Fascists were everywhere. Your father had gone into hiding, making his way to Portugal. He had a job offer in America, and was waiting for us. I was supposed to join him in Lisbon, but was very pregnant with your sister and could not travel. I had the two little boys with me. By the time she was born and I was able to travel, it had become impossible to get exit papers.

We, your grandparents, your father, and I, were all very worried. I decided to kill the children if they came to arrest us. I had bought poison pills for this purpose. Or perhaps I would send them away into the countryside with our Italian maid. I had already been called in for questioning and had no travel papers.

There was a glamorous Italian woman who lived in our building. Everyone despised her because she often was seen with high-ranking Fascist officials. Almost a prostitute, people thought. I sort of liked her though; she was high-spirited and funny and had beautiful clothes. We were always cordial to each another. One day, soon after your sister was born, she saw me crying in our building's common area. What's wrong, she asked. I am a Jew. I'm afraid we'll all be killed, my children with me. I have no papers and cannot leave. She laughed, rather affectionately, almost teasingly. Oh, is that your problem. Don't worry, I can get your papers for you easily from one of my friends. And so she did.

What struck me so much about this story? Terror; for years I dreamed the Nazis would come and get me. Even more starkly, the unimaginable idea that my mother would kill her children, us, me. And then there was the mystery, the statement that rang out so sharply. "I am a Jew." What did that mean? I knew my mother was Catholic, as was my father. We went to Church every Sunday.

From these beginnings to my own well-established Jewish identity is not the story I tell here. What does preoccupy me is the role of story-telling itself as the fixed point in the establishment of Jewish identity. (We have only to look at the Hebrew Bible!) The point here is that our family history, officially that of a pro-

https://doi.org/10.1515/9783110731965-003

lific American Catholic family, my father a leading scholar of medieval canon law, had a subtext of something quite different, something hidden, dangerous, indeed life-threatening, and immensely powerful. We were Jews. Whatever that meant.

Introduction

In the fields with which we are concerned,
knowledge comes only in lightning flashes.
The text is the long roll of thunder that follows.
– Walter Benjamin, The Arcades Project

Personal chronicles are like lightning flashes
that illuminate parts of a landscape.
– Saul Friedländer, The Years of Extermination

German Jews and the Persistence of Jewish Identity in Conversion: Writing the Jewish Self is a book about the fraught aftermath of the conversionary impulse among modernizing German Jews. Its focus is on an insistent Jewish identity as it plays out in the liminal space of the converted German Jew, a space of fluid, often indistinct contours, haunted by historical trauma and a bygone culture, obsessed by the urgent need to reformulate a sense of self. Structured around personal narratives in written and oral form, the book is simultaneously about continuity and discontinuity, contiguity and fragmentation, the shards of self drawn into the gravitational pull of a distant culture, a people, a fate, of Jewishness itself.

Specifically, *Writing the Jewish Self* revolves around the story of one family, my family, as it grapples with the meaning of its fateful Jewish origins in a post-Holocaust, post-conversionary milieu. As the Jewish daughter of German Jewish refugees, 1930s converts to Roman Catholicism, my interest in this topic is both academic and deeply personal, as reflected in the book's focus, trajectory, and, hopefully, crossover appeal. My inquiry is situated at the interface of history, memory, and life writing (and, in its contemporary guise, the oral history interview), and their combined impact on the complexities of my family of hybrid, postmodern Jews whose reality, I argue, defies categorization and the dismissive politics of naming and shaming. My medium of analysis is the text as site for the performance of identity, which in turn becomes the construction of identity. My texts originate within my converted parents' oh-so-different stories and their refracted trajectory within the over two dozen videotaped interviews I conducted with two generations of their many descendants. Within these rich multiple sources, I seek to ascertain the impact of a contested Jewish identity on the deconstruction and reconstruction of the Jewish self. I offer my texts as "lightning flashes that illuminate parts of a landscape," my commentary, "the long roll of thunder that follows," the whole playing its part in the endless refashioning that can be said to drive the Jewish text and Jewish history itself.

https://doi.org/10.1515/9783110731965-004

For inspiration I turn, among others, to Jacques Derrida's insistence on the destabilizing, even dangerous possibilities of archive[1] and to Walter Benjamin's insistence on history as "montage."[2] I also draw on Cynthia Baker's brilliant historical exegesis of the word *Jew* and her persuasive argument, emphatically rejecting traditional ethnic and religious constructs, that "the name *Jew* defies all claims to proper possession or exclusive ownership."[3] I am also inspired by Leslie Morris's brilliant re-imagining, in *The Translated Jew,* written in the wake of Naomi Seidman's imposing scholarship, of the notion of translation as a fluid, polysemic space, occurring at the level of the individual, allowing new possibilities and meanings to emerge and collide. "I posit Jewishness as the sign that is always about to be deciphered, yet it is never fully deciphered," she insists,[4] positioning translation, conceptualized as endless re-writing, endless re-imagining, at the very core of the Jewish enterprise.[5] The insights of these and other scholars inform and inspire my own explorations into the nature and persistence of Jewish identity in conversion, my family serving as resource and paradigm.

By way of this brief Introduction, I seek to situate my family history within the larger story of the role of conversion in the fraught German Jewish encounter with modernity. As literary antecedent, because this is a book about *Writing the Jewish Self,* I invoke the convert Rahel Varnhagen, born Rahel Levin, endlessly reformulating and revisiting in her highly charged correspondence the anguish of her liminal status. I also introduce the figure of the Marrano, not as historical antecedent, but rather as archetype or perhaps metaphor[6] for the ambiguities of the vexed identity emerging from conversion. Finally, I provide a brief roadmap to the many voices that constitute the core of the exploration I undertake here: *Writing the Jewish Self.*

---

1 Jacques Derrida, *Archive Fever: A Freudian Impression,* trans. Eric Prenowitz (Chicago: University of Chicago Press, 1996).

2 See, e.g., Walter Benjamin, *The Arcades Project,* trans. Howard Eiland and Kevin McLaughlin (Cambridge, MA: Belknap, 1999), 461.

3 Cynthia M. Baker, *Jew* (New Brunswick, NJ: Rutgers University Press, 2016), 9.

4 Leslie Morris, *The Translated Jew* (Evanston, Ill.: Northwestern University Press, 2018), 18; see also Naomi Seidman, *Faithful Renderings* (Chicago: University of Chicago Press, 2006), 10.

5 Morris, 25.

6 As in Elaine Marks's provocative title, *Marrano as Metaphor* (New York: Columbia University Press, 1996), an analysis of the fraught valences of Jewishness and Judaism in French literature.

The Conversion Phenomenon: A Historical Perspective

The appearance of an unprecedented number of conversions to Christianity among modernizing German Jews in the so-called *Taufepidemie,* originating almost simultaneously with Moses Mendelssohn's late eighteenth-century pioneering Enlightenment initiative (famously, four of his six children converted), has been well documented.[7] Several statistical analyses of the demographics of conversion for the period, primarily in Berlin, broadly agree on a sharp rise in the first part of the nineteenth century, with rates sharply declining after 1850 and then spiking again, briefly, in the period following German unification in 1870.[8] All sources agree that social cohesion with non-Jews, even for converts, remained largely problematic.[9]

The historiographical and ideological debate over the meaning of these trends reveals a continuum of attitudes over time.[10] Thus, until the late nineteenth century, the German Jewish conversion phenomenon was harshly judged, frequently exaggerated, and largely marginalized as a source for authentic Jewish history. In the early twentieth century, the new field of Jewish social science linked conversion (and intermarriage) to statistics on crime, disease, and mental illness, reflecting a then-Zionist perspective on diaspora Judaism as a doomed and degenerate enterprise. Nonetheless, as Todd Endelman perceptively points out, these early twentieth-century studies constitute a "demarginalization" of conversion, the convert now become an integral if not essential component of the Jewish emancipation project and no longer an outlier. To Endelman, then, Jewish conversion, or what he calls "radical assimilation," constitutes an ex-

---

7 See. e. g. Deborah Hertz, *How Jews Became Germans* (New Haven, Conn.: Yale University Press, 2007); *Jewish High Society in Old Regime Berlin* (Syracuse: Syracuse University Press, 2005); Steven M. Lowenstein, *The Berlin Jewish Community* (New York: Oxford University Press, 1994).
8 Lowenstein and Hertz, using different methodologies to examine overlapping periods, together estimate the number of conversions in Berlin between 1770 and 1874 at about seven percent, a remarkably stable ratio that arguably belies the concept of *"Taufepidemie."* Hertz, *Jewish High Society,* 232; *How Jews Became Germans,* 223; Lowenstein, 7–8, 121–122.
9 See Warner E. Mosse, *The German–Jewish Economic Elite, 1820–1935: A Socio-Cultural Profile* (New York: Oxford University Press, 1989); David Sorkin, *The Transformation of German Jewry: 1780–1840* (Detroit: Wayne State University Press, 1999); Marion A. Kaplan, *The Making of the Jewish Middle Class* (Oxford: Oxford University Press, 1991); "Unter Uns: Jews Socializing with other Jews in Imperial Germany," *Leo Baeck Institute Yearbook* 48 (2003), 41–65.
10 See Todd Endelman, "Welcoming Ex-Jews in the Jewish Historiographical Fold," in *The Margins of Jewish History,* ed. Marc Lee Raphael (Williamsburg, VA: Department of Religion, The College of William and Mary, 2000), 14–22, for a fine review of the historical scholarship. My summaries are drawn from this work.

treme response to acculturation differing in degree but not in kind from the response of other German Jews to recurrent waves of discriminatory, anti-Jewish, and antisemitic pressures in modernity.[11]

While Endelman has devoted the bulk of his career to a largely sociological exploration of the phenomenon of modern Jewish conversion, primarily in Germany but also beyond,[12] his work essentially stops at the baptismal font. My work, in contrast, shines a spotlight on what happens after, what happens to the Jew within. While numerous eminent historians, as set forth in brief below, have deconstructed the early modern world of the Marrano, with the exception of Ellie Schainker's recent, well-received study of Jewish converts in Imperial Russia (which concludes that conversion did not mark the end of their Jewishness),[13] little if any work has been done on the world of the converted German Jew. Using a cross-disciplinary methodology incorporating text, interview materials, and wide-ranging theories of critical analysis, and focusing on the personal to illuminate a complex historical phenomenon, I propose here a new cultural history that challenges conventional boundaries of what is Jewish and what is not.

The Literary Context: The Jew in Flux

I reach back to Rahel Varnhagen (1771–1833), whose voluminous correspondence with the leading intellectual, cultural, and political luminaries of her time offers an incisive and moving portrait of the deeply felt anxieties of this idiosyncratic, brilliant pioneer rushing headlong into the intellectual and cultural ferment of a dawning modernity. Unable to resolve the strictures and stigma inherent in her wealthy Jewish birth, desperate to fully participate in the challenges of a new era, her repeated self-naming and re-naming can be seen as acts of deconstruction and reconstruction in her unavailing efforts to free herself from the stringent social disabilities of her Jewish and gendered status. Ultimately to become Antonie Frederike Varnhagen von Ense in her final, post-conversion, post-marriage incarnation, she remained known to all, iconically, ironically, as "Rahel."[14]

---

11 Endelman, "Welcoming Ex-Jews," 16.

12 Endelman, *Leaving the Jewish Fold: Conversion and Radical Assimilation in Modern Jewish History* (Princeton: Princeton University Press, 2015).

13 See, generally, Ellie R. Schainker, *Confessions of the Shtetl: Converts from Judaism in Imperial Russia, 1817–1906* (Stanford: Stanford University Press, 2016).

14 For detailed, nuanced, and highly readable accounts of the period, see Hertz, *How Jews Became Germans;* see also her earlier *Jewish High Society in Old Regime Berlin*, originally published by Yale University Press in 1988. The account below is based principally on Hertz's work. See

Indeed it begins and ends with a name. Rahel. Everyone in turn-of-the-century Berlin high society knew who she was. The brilliant, fascinating, "exotic" Rahel Levin, salonière extraordinaire, whose glittering "open houses" attracted a heady and altogether new mash-up of prominent intellectuals and artists, non-Jews and Jews, men and women, nobles and commoners, publishers, writers, and actors. An ever-evolving cohort, passionately engaged in discussing the latest literary provocations of Goethe, Rousseau, and other contemporary cultural icons of the Romantic era, all deeply aware of the dawning of a new age, a new culture, and a new identity for Germany, each determined to play a role in what was then seen as a deeply progressive force. And the most brilliant among these many brilliant conversationalists, by acclamation almost, was Rahel herself, renowned for the originality and subtlety of her conversation and an equally legendary largesse of spirit and heart. As the name indicates (the first of her many names), Rahel Levin was a Jew, a "Jewess" specifically, a term that vibrates in the cultural orbit then as now. How could a "Jewess" be at the epicenter of the Berlin intellectual and social universe?

With difficulty. The crevices and contradictions in this entirely new way of being (the term "lifestyle" had not yet been invented) were to dominate her life. Born into a wealthy, worldly banking family, managing to escape her family's pressure for an early, financially advantageous Jewish marriage, already at age twenty Rahel was to proclaim, "I shall never be convinced that I am a Schlemiehl and a Jewess."[15] Like many members of her intimate circle, she sought to cement her newly gained intellectual and social freedom in a marriage into the nobility.[16] Following a pair of presumptive (and disastrous) "engagements" in her late twenties and early thirties,[17] Rahel finally was to marry, at age forty-

---

also Hannah Arendt, *Rahel Varnhagen: The Life of a Jewess*, ed. Liliane Weissberg, trans. Richard and Clara Winston (Baltimore: The Johns Hopkins University Press, 1907) for a seminal deconstruction and interpretation of Rahel Varnhagen's life and work.

15 Arendt, 89, 288; see ibid., 283 for Weissberg's citation methodology.

16 See Hertz, *Jewish High Society*, 191, 222. Indeed, seven of her nine fellow Berlin Jewish salonières, among them Dorothea Mendelssohn, did marry noblemen, often in second marriages. Ibid., 191–192. These marriages required conversion to Christianity, civil marriage being unavailable in Prussia until 1874. Ibid., 208. In Hertz's incisive analysis, for a brief period that coincided with the heyday of the Berlin Jewish salons (1780–1806), the social interests of the wealthy Jewish salonières and the financial interests of the (relatively) impoverished younger sons of the landed aristocracy converged, both parties having something to gain. Ibid., 214.

17 She finally broke off the first affair, with a Count Karl von Finckenstein, after four years during which he never introduced her to his family. Hertz, *How Jews Became Germans*, 54. The second, with a handsome Spanish diplomat, Don Raphael d'Urquijo, ended with this crude and

three, Karl Auguste Varnhagen, a man of relatively insignificant origins, who through unstinting effort managed to climb from his rather humble beginnings as a tutor to a wealthy Jewish family to a series of military and adjunct positions, eventually gaining for himself a Prussian diplomatic post.[18] Once there, he managed (somewhat dubiously) to invent for himself a title (von Ense).[19] Armed at last with a title and a respectable income, Varnhagen finally was able to marry Rahel in 1814 (their affair had begun in 1808),[20] a date that coincided with her conversion.[21] Thus her rather cavalier *bon mot*, "As long as one nobleman exists, one must also be ennobled,"[22] concealed both a steely resolve and an acute, unhappy understanding of the innate limitations of her circumstances and her era.[23]

What then is the significance of Rahel Varnhagen to the focus and thrust of this book? I suggest three lenses with which to consider the unique achievements of this remarkable woman.

First, as Deborah Hertz suggests, the salonières in general, in their embrace of the wider cultural and intellectual narratives of their time and their society, represent an early, family-based solution to the challenge of modernity with gender at the fore.[24]

Second is the literary form itself in which Rahel recorded her unhappy struggle. Choosing an inherently fragmented form, reveling in an almost madcap prolixity (she was to write an estimated 10,000 letters, of which some 6,000 are pre-

highly undiplomatic rejection: "What do you want, Finck already treated you this way, this should not be anything new to you." Arendt, 156, 325, see also, ibid., 150–156.

18 Detailed, variously in Hertz, *How Jews became Germans*, 61, 116–117, 124–126 and Arendt, 194–204, 225–238. Arendt's disdain for Varnhagen throughout is obvious.

19 Hertz, *How Jews Became Germans*, 124.

20 Ibid., 73.

21 See note 16 above.

22 Cited in Arendt, 227, 352 (Weissberg note) dating the comment as 1809.

23 The period's unremitting antisemitism and open misogyny is captured by a remark of Wilhelm von Humboldt, the foremost intellectual and diplomat of his day. A frequent and enthusiastic participant in Rahel's salon in the 1790s, later to become a noted proponent of Jewish emancipation at the 1815 Congress of Vienna, von Humboldt nonetheless was to comment "I was told that … [Varnhagen] has now married the little Levy. Thus she was able now to become an ambassador's wife and excellency. There is not anything which cannot be achieved by a Jew." Cited in Hertz, *How Jews*, 125.

24 Hertz, *Jewish High Society*, xx. Elsewhere Hertz sees conversion among the salonières as "a functional, makeshift, problematic substitute for emancipation," arguing against a simplistic model of opportunism versus loyalty. Hertz, *How Jews*, 218.

served),[25] Rahel's writing for all its brilliance resembles nothing so much as the glittering shards of a broken mirror. A constant refrain runs throughout: the letter writer's impassioned insistence that her ultimate failure to be admitted to the first-tier ranks of Germany's turn-of-the century intellectual class is due to her gendered and Jewish status.[26]

Finally, of course, her conversion itself, epitomized in her final radical self-renaming, can be seen as an embodied, futile attempt to escape from the stigma of Otherness and illustrates its power and durability as well as its centrality to periods of rapid historical change. As Rahel was to remark in a late letter to her younger friend, litterateur, and notorious fellow convert, Heinrich Heine, "only galley slaves know one another."[27]

The Marrano in Modernity[28]

Prominent historians have noted the "lure of the Sephardic" in the Jewish Enlightenment and beyond.[29] Mendelssohn's followers had seized upon Sephardim as examples of Jews who were able to combine a Judaism noteworthy for its cul-

---

25 Amos Elon, *The Pity of It All* (New York: Henry Holt and Company, 2002), 78. See also Hertz, *Jewish High Society*, xv-xvi for the archival history.

26 As Hertz puts it in a moving epilogue, "When I judged the converts critically ... I stood firmly within the Jewish world, lamenting the departure of a member of the tribe. But when I sympathized with a convert, I stood as a modern cosmopolitan, celebrating self-definition and the audacity to shape one's own destiny." Hertz, *How Jews*, 220.

27 Cited in Arendt, 258. Famously writing of his baptism as "an admission ticket to European culture," Heine was destined to live out his pre-conversion conviction that "the Jew can never be washed off," an obvious allusion to baptism. A controversial figure reviled and embraced both in his lifetime and to this day, an Outsider's Outsider, he can be seen as a prototype of the modern Marrano and as such of the complex and vexing issue of Jewish hybridity and a modern multiplicity of identities. For a detailed treatment, see Angela Botelho, "Modern Marranism and the German-Jewish Experience: The Persistence of Jewish Identity in Conversion," Master's Thesis, Graduate Theological Union, 2013, Berkeley California, 11–43.

28 My discovery of the Marrano occurred in my very first post-career class in Jewish Studies. Prior to that moment, I had never known a Jew outside of my own family who had been baptized. The resultant shock led me over time directly to this very book.

29 Ismar Schorsch, "The Myth of Sephardic Supremacy," *Leo Baeck Institute Yearbook* 14 (1989), 47–66, 49. See also, Jonathan Skolnick, *Jewish Pasts, German Fictions: History, Memory, and Minority Culture in Germany, 1824–1955* (Stanford: Stanford University Press, 2014). For the Marrano's powerful grip on the nineteenth-century German Jewish bourgeois imagination and beyond, see John M. Efron, *German Jewry and the Allure of the Sephardic* (Princeton: Princeton University Press, 2016), seeing the nineteenth-century German Jewish cultural obsession with the Sephardic devolving at times into a disparaging rejection of its actual shared Ashkenazic past.

tural and poetic production with full participation in an integrated high culture. In Ismar Schorsch's perceptive analysis, the embrace of the Sephardic myth, "coloured by social need," supported the rebellion against the Ashkenazi culture from which German Jewry had sprung while serving to "ground institutional rebellion in Jewish soil" and thus mitigate the tensions inherent in a modernizing German Jewry's "discontinuity with historical roots."[30] However, as dreams of cultural integration failed to materialize, interest shifted to the Marranos, particularly to figures like Uriel da Costa and Baruch Spinoza, as all too relevant examples of the conflict between a traditional rabbinic Judaism and a modern, enlightened, freethinking sensibility.[31]

The outward contours of the Marrano experience are well-known.[32] Beginning with the forced mass conversions of 1391 in Spain and the later conversion by decree in Portugal, many Jews were repositioned as New Christians, *conversos* or, more pejoratively, Marranos.[33] Generally prosperous, politically successful, largely socially and culturally cohesive, the Marranos became influential throughout Iberia despite the persistence of discriminatory practices and assorted internal tensions. Mid-century, however, brought a growing backlash, marked by a fear of secret "Judaizing" and a growing obsession with *limpieza de sangre* (purity of blood).[34] In 1478 the Spanish Inquisition launched an era of overt persecution largely focused on the Marranos. After the Spanish expulsion of the Jews in 1492, many Marranos fled to Portugal where they became a large and well-organized force, highly active in commerce and interna-

---

30 Schorsch, "Myth," 47–48. To Schorsch, the "fascination with Spain that comes to characterize the German Jewish scene comes to dominate Jewish life in fields as diverse as liturgy, architecture, literature, and scholarship." Ibid., 48; see also 53–66.
31 Michael A. Meyer, *Judaism Within Modernity: Essays on Jewish History and Religion* (Detroit: Wayne State University Press, 2001), 46–47 and note 6; ibid., *Jewish Identity in the Modern World* (London: University of London Press, 1990), 14–15 and note 10. See also, David Biale, *Not In the Heavens: The Tradition of Jewish Secular Thought* (Princeton: Princeton University Press, 2011), 34–35.
32 Classic Marrano histories include Yizhak Baer, *History of the Jews in Christian Spain* (Philadelphia: Jewish Publication Society of America,1966); Salo Baron, *A Social and Religious History of the Jews*, vol. 15 (New York: Columbia University Press, 1973); Cecil Roth, *A History of the Marranos*, 4th ed. (New York: Harmon Press, 1974). Among the later generation of scholars, see also, Miriam Bodian, *Hebrews of the Portuguese Nation* (Bloomington: Indiana University Press, 1997); Yosef Yerushalmi, *From Spanish Court to Italian Ghetto* (Seattle: London: University of Washington Press, 1971).
33 Initially derogatory, (Marrano means pig), the term became generic.
34 See, generally, Yirmiyahu Yovel, *Spinoza and Other Heretics: The Marrano of Reason* (Princeton: Princeton University Press, 1989), 15–17; ibid., *The Other Within* (Princeton: Princeton University Press, 2009), 57.

tional trade.[35] Once the Portuguese Inquisition took hold around 1580, Portuguese Marranos, many of Spanish origin, began emigrating to Northern Europe, especially to Amsterdam with its reputation of intellectual and religious tolerance. There they formed a recast "Portuguese Nation," intent on recapturing their former prominence in international trade and commerce, and, for many, equally intent on reconstituting a Judaism that had been largely suppressed or lost.[36] A strong countercultural phenomenon of dissidence emerged as well, epitomized most notably by Baruch Spinoza, the radical rationalist philosopher and political theorist, and also by his lesser-known predecessor, Uriel da Costa. As noted above, both figured prominently in the imaginations of nineteenth-century German Jewish pioneers of modernity.

The Marrano experience of boundary-crossing, marginality, and trauma remembered or suppressed has long engendered an oft divisive discourse on the nature of Jewish identity,[37] and one that holds particular appeal to me. I focus here on the analysis of Yirmiyahu Yovel as particularly relevant to my own family's conversion experience. In his path-breaking study, *Spinoza and Other Heretics*, Yovel finds in the ambivalence and conflicted self-identity of the Marrano a harbinger of modernity, arguing that the Marranos who fled to Holland and elsewhere re-experienced the duality and the alienation inherent in their Iberian origins in new form. He posits, then, that the noted seventeenth-century Amsterdam dissidents, above all Baruch Spinoza, exemplify the classic Marrano experience of duality and alienation transformed into rationalism, skepticism, and a pre-modern secularism.[38] Expanding on his thesis in *The Other Within*, Yovel argues that what he sees as the Marrano's emblematic traits anticipate major trends of Western modernity in general and Jewish modernity in particular.[39] I myself have argued, in an unpublished master's thesis that lies at the origin of the present work, that the phenomenon Yovel describes transcends the period in which it originated, living on in what I called "modern marranism" among German Jews, particularly those who converted, and their descendants.[40]

---

35 Yerushami, 3–12.

36 Bodian, *Hebrews*, 96–131; Yosef Kaplan, "Bom Judesmo," in *Cultures of the Jews: A New History*, ed. David Biale (New York: Schocken Books, 2002), 337–367; Yerushalmi, 31–33.

37 See notes 32, 34.

38 Yovel, *Spinoza*, 26–38.

39 Yovel, *The Other Within*, 337–377; see 330–339 (identifying twenty-three traits). Yovel goes on to opine that the modernization of Ashkenazi Jews demonstrates "interesting links of analogy and precedent" to the Marrano past, remaining careful to postulate structural similarities rather than causality.

40 Botelho, "Modern Marranism," 6–20.

As a paradigm of modernity, then, the Marrano, or modern marranism, speaks to the dislocations of Jewish identity, particularly among German Jews, while paradoxically affirming the continued vitality of that identity in all its rich variability.

A Road Map

Against this rich background, I present, in Part I, "My Very Own Converts: A Diptych," a portrait of my two very different parents, Eva and Stephan Kuttner.

The first chapter, "A Mother's Tale," revolves around my eighty-four-year-old mother's 1998 "Sort of Autobiography." Written shortly after her husband's death, her memoir focuses almost exclusively on her hair-raising escape from the Nazis almost sixty years earlier with three young children in tow, an escape tale obsessively retold to each of her nine children and eighteen grandchildren, a story I call "our own personal Haggadah." Remarkable in its blend of the intimate, replete with cultural resonance (signifying the German Jewish obsession with *Bildung*) alongside the horrific (her elderly grandmother's deportation, suicide pills, cattle cars), the written narrative immediately grips us with its strong forward thrust. Writing to preserve "your family history" (her emphasis), she has made sure that her legacy is preserved in her own personal act of *Zakhor*. In it, and in the countless oral iterations that precede it, I find a compelling source of post-conversion Jewish identity in our family.

In Chapter 2, I present a reading of my father Stephan Kuttner as "Hidden Jew." His Jewishness obscured in the brilliant trajectory of his rise to prominence as a world-renowned scholar in the rarefied field of medieval canon law, he himself already the son of a convert to the state religion, my father followed a path of many deracinated German Jews of the Weimar era seeking to resolve postwar disillusionment and a renewed search for meaning in conversion, in his case to Roman Catholicism. There he forged a brilliant academic career in which his Judaism remained obscured. And yet, I argue, as a prime example of an exceptional European culture, committed to learning in all its guises, my father continued to epitomize the German Jew par excellence. Indeed, I find in my father's very commitment to canon law as the focal point of an elevated spiritual and social ideal the core of the basic Jewish enterprise. Faith as law, law as faith: this is where I find my deeply hidden Jewish father.

Part II, "Resonances," deconstructs in two chapters the twenty-five oral history interviews I conducted of two generations of my converted parents' descendants. Set forth in transcribed excerpts, each of my interviewees, almost all raised non-Jewishly, all but one untethered from a Catholicism long since all but abandoned, discuss their relationship to their Jewish ancestry and to a Jewish identity. Their stories reveal the deep impact of my mother's Jewish escape story, the effect of my father's scholarly commitments, and, more often than not, a deeply-felt cultural affinity to the world of the emancipated German Jew, weaving a complex pattern of transmission.

Chapter 3, "Sibling Stories: In Search of the Authentic Self," engages the recent voices of my seven living siblings, who, like myself, experienced most directly and intimately the full impact of our converted German Jewish parents' presentation of self. Each of us reflected deeply on our own evolving identities as we had groped our way through our liminal family landscape to emerge at the margins of Jewish identity, surprisingly and perhaps not so surprisingly, more often than not claiming a proud Jewish inheritance and a Jewish self.

In Chapter 4, "The Third Generation: Points of Light," I explore a number of overlapping themes arising out of my many third-generation interviews with those who knew their well-loved German Jewish grandparents at a remove and yet were strongly marked by them. Indeed, by the time they reached full adulthood, which is when I interviewed them, almost all had begun to reclaim in one way or another a Jewish heritage and a form of Jewish identity; the Catholic overlay had all but disappeared. Their idiosyncratic voices, linked by a shared conflicted background, reflect not only the multiplicity and fragmentation characteristic of the landscape of the postmodern Jew, so beautifully theorized in the work of Baker and Morris, they also reinforce for me the dominant theme of my work; that is, the near impossibility of conversion, of being born again, as a project involving Jews.

Part I

My Very Own Converts: A Diptych

"The Challenge of a Usable Past"[1]

How apt, it seems to me, to evoke the Leo Baeck Institute in my borrowed quotation as I focus on texts that inform my view of my converted German Jewish parents' divergent responses to their Jewish past. Their self-presentations vary dramatically. As we shall see, my mother throughout her life continued to transmit in startling outbursts a compelling, urgent message, an unmistakably *Jewish* message, stark and highly personalized, emphatically demanding our attention. My reticent father, in contrast, leaves little more than his vast body of scholarship for us to trace a connection to his Jewish past. Yet, I argue, by my reading, his work betrays an elusive yet unmistakable Jewish presence, manifested in his embrace of law as the ultimate spiritual and religious act.[2]

The thrust of these two chapters inexorably leads me to the issue of my own reconstruction of the past. In speaking of the persistence of Jewish identity in the trajectory of my deceased parents' lives, I am writing, after all, about subjects who can no longer respond, disagree, or argue with an analysis that may well have been provocative to them. I am reminded of Jacques Derrida's brilliant analysis of Yosef Yerushalmi's celebrated attempt, based on newly uncovered archival material (a letter from Jakob Freud to his son Sigmund on the occasion of the latter's thirty-fifth birthday), to impose a defining Jewish identity not only on a notoriously recalcitrant subject, Sigmund Freud, but also on the psychoanalytic project itself as Freud conceived of it.[3] Freud is dead, objects Derrida, and can only acquiesce.[4] Derrida thus describes Yerushalmi's celebrated interpretation of Freud as a specifically Jewish and extraordinary act of *violence* [my italics],

---

1 I borrow this quotation from the title of the 2018 Annual Conference of the Leo Baeck Institute.

2 See Chaya Halberstam, "Wisdom, *Torah, Nomos:* The Discursive Contours of Biblical Law," Sage Publications, 2013. http://journals.sagepub.com/doi/10.1177/1743872111404174 (accessed July 14, 2018).

3 Jacques Derrida, *Archive Fever: A Freudian Impression,* trans. Eric Prenowitz (Chicago: University of Chicago Press, 1996); see generally, Yosef Yerushalmi, *Freud's Moses: Judaism Terminable and Interminable* (New Haven: Yale University Press, 1991). While Yerushalmi strategically denies any claim to psychoanalysis as "Jewish," he also undercuts his own disclaimer, slyly suggesting that Freud may have thought so. See Yerushalmi, *Freud's Moses* xxii; compare ibid., 84, evoking "the core of your analogy between the development of religious tradition and that of individual neurosis."

4 Derrida, *Archive Fever,* 41.

https://doi.org/10.1515/9783110731965-005

analogous to circumcision, he goes on to argue, as a brutal, painful inscription on a non-responding, because incapable of responding, subject.[5]

It is telling that Derrida's critique of Yerushalmi takes place in the context of his extended essay, the aptly titled *Archive Fever* [*Mal d'Archive*].[6] To Derrida, the archive itself [7] as concept and as practice directly impinges on and destabilizes the concept of history and historiography. On the one hand, he says, traditionally the archive operates as a device to fix memory, to impose order upon the past, to fix or freeze time. On the other, as an opening into the practice of history, and more indirectly into the science of historiography, the archive remains in essence endlessly fluid and open to the future, to new interpretations.[8] Thus, he reminds us, the archive participates in both past and future, in French, *l'avenir*, or *a-venir*, that which is to come.[9]

This then is my practice in combing through my deceased parents' texts. I seek to destabilize the official account of an exemplary Catholic family, nine children, Catholic scholar father, resourceful stay-at-home mother, memorialized, to our acute discomfort, in a local newspaper article, complete with a grainy photograph, in the early 1950s. In its place I interpose a different story, the backstory of an externally *and* internally displaced family of German Jews, dually exiled. In so doing I seek to expand the meaning of what it means to be a Jew, or perhaps more accurately, of what Jewishness can come to mean in the aftermath of conversion, by exploring its archival afterimage, literally even, in the case of the videotaped interviews of my parent's many descendants. Merriam-Webster defines "afterimage" as "a usually visual sensation occurring after stimulation by its external cause has ceased." I myself turn to words, my parent's words, and those of their children and grandchildren, redefined as archives in the Derridean sense, to find a resonance, a lingering echo, to turn to

---

5 Derrida, 41–42.

6 The French title is brilliantly translated here, evoking as it does both illness and obsession. In Derrida's expansive description, the *Mal d'Archive* functions as "a compulsive, repetitive, and nostalgic desire for the archive, an irrepressible desire to return to the origin, a homesickness, a nostalgia for the return to the most archaic place of absolute commencement." Ibid., 91. Could this be an apt description of my own project?

7 The term is broadly conceived here to include emails, letters, indeed the products of all sorts of technological advance. Ibid., 17–18. It obviously would include, I would argue, the transcripts of the recorded interviews that inform the final two chapters of my manuscript.

8 As Derrida summarizes, to the delight of all historians I would surmise, "The archivist produces more archive, and that is why the archive is never closed. It opens out of the future." Ibid., 68.

9 Ibid.

another sense organ, of Jewishness after its "stimulation by its external cause," namely a formal adherence to a Jewish polity, has ceased.

I must then in all honesty own the violence of my act of naming the Jew who continues to abide within the two very disparate people who are my convert parents and whom I call out in this portion of my work. And yet, as Jorge Luis Borges suggestively intimates, "every writer *creates* his own precursors. His work modifies our conception of the past, as it will modify the future."[10] It is within this context, as well as within Derrida's vision of the unavoidable dual nature of archive, that I situate my own efforts to understand the world of the converted German Jew and the convoluted persistence of a Jewish identity within that liminal space through the urgent, oft ambivalent, always challenging family voices I call forth here and below. Like Borges, I hope to deepen our understanding of a particular kind of Jewish past, the German Jew in conversion, as well to as to open up, through the interviews that follow in the second part of this piece, the potential for creativity and porousness in our notions of Jewish identity, beckoning towards our common, postmodern future, the *a-venir.*

---

10 Jorge Luis Borges, *Labyrinths*, "Kafka and His Precursors," trans. by James E. Irby (New York: New Directions Publishing Corporation, 2007), 199 – 201, 201.

1 A Mother's Tale

In 1998, at the age of 84,[1] two years after the death of her husband of some sixty-five years, my mother Eva Kuttner, a German Jewish refugee, youthful convert to Roman Catholicism on the eve of her marriage to my father, painstakingly typed up a brief autobiographical sketch, just six pages long, for her children. Calling it "a sort of autobiography," and, simultaneously, "your family history" [emphasis in the original], writing, "to amuse you all – so here it goes," she launches into her story.[2]

> Oma[3] always told me "you were a complete surprise we were happy with our 3 children, we had a son – and then you came along, not even a brother for Ludwig, and just when I wanted to read the newspaper (I was born a few days after the beginning of world war one) I wanted to name you Susanne (Figaro) but your father confessed he still had nightmares about his childhood nurse by that name, so we settled for Eva (Meistersinger) All that never fazed me – it seemed just amusing to me – this optimistic nature I inherited from my grandmother (Oma's mother)[4] who, when she was deported in October 1941 at the age of 84[5] "confessed" to Frl. Greinert, my mother's best friend who sent her off at the trainstation where cattlecars were used to transport the mostly old people to Theresienstadt "(Terezin)" that she could not bring herself to use the suicide pills she was given by a friend (her Doctor?) "because I think something good might still happen to me." [6]

This amazing document reminds me so much of my mother! The galloping pace, the hairpin turns, the jokiness, the boundless optimism, and then, the sharply intruding, incredibly dangerous dark side—cattle cars, suicide pills, deportation, death—all recollected as "your family history."[7] And all of this in the very first paragraph!

Striking in its blend of the intimate and the horrific, this astonishing debut immediately grips us with its strong forward thrust. Replete with cultural reso-

---

1 Internally dated ("4 years ago, I think it was in 1994"). See Appendix I (original complete text), 143 – 148, 145.
2 App. I, 143.
3 Our maternal grandmother. I retain throughout this chapter my mother's original spelling, punctuation, orthography, and parenthetical expressions.
4 I cannot allow her to remain nameless; her name was Dora Ullmann.
5 My mother is mistaken in a couple of minor details. Born in 1861, Dora Ulman was actually eighty-one when she was deported on October 7, 1942 (not 1941). She died less than three weeks later, on October 20, 1942. See Chapter 3, 65. Perhaps my mother conflated her mother's lifespan with her own?
6 App, I, 143.
7 Ibid.

https://doi.org/10.1515/9783110731965-006

nance (naming choices dictated by Mozart's and Wagner's operatic heroines, signifiers of the German Jewish obsession with *Bildung*)[8] slammed up against grimly detailed reality (a grandmother's deportation "at the age of 84," "cattle cars," "suicide pills," a friend's witnessing of the engines of transport), it manages, all unselfconsciously, to encapsulate the entire history of the German Jews. Birth and death are linked to an astonishing optimism against all odds in face of the brutal intrusions of history, war at the one end of the paragraph, deportation at the other. "Something good might still happen to me," my great-grandmother reportedly says as she is forced onto the cattle car en route to her final destination, Theresienstadt. Survival as optimism, against a specifically Jewish backdrop and the intermittent horrors of Jewish history, an optimism that will resurface later as "luck"[9]—is this the stance my mother so urgently wished to pass on to us in the midst of this dark tale, highlighted so vigorously in her very first paragraph?

What follows for the next two and a half pages is a warm portrait of the comfortably secular, upper middle-class German Jewish culture of the Weimar era, the recollected German Jewish "bourgeois world of that time" with its cook, its maid, and its governess,[10] so glamorous to a young American child amid the refugee family's straitened circumstances. Teasing the maid, harassing the governess, these were her childhood pleasures; along with *Struwelpeter*, Anderson's fairy tales, *Vati*'s birthday poems,[11] all strikingly non-Jewish. Altogether, a "happy protected childhood," tragically disrupted by a brother's death in 1926 in what my mother, then aged eleven, experienced as childhood's end.[12] The solution for a bereaved Oma reads as a typical *Bildung* project; she launches into a translation of French books into German, among them Maurice Maeterlinck's just-published *The Life of the Termites*.[13] The well-received translation project continues from 1926 to the fateful date of 1933, my mother tells us, but does not spell out why it ended. Does my mother assume that we would know? Flashes of humor run throughout: my grandfather's dry wit ("After her first book ap-

---

8 App. I, 143. The literature on the complex German Jewish involvement with *Bildung* is vast. I reference here two seminal studies, both brief and eminently readable: Paul Mendes-Flohr, *German Jews: A Dual Identity* (New Haven: Yale University Press, 1999); George L. Mosse, *German Jews Beyond Judaism* (Bloomington: Indiana University Press, 1984).
9 App. I, 146.
10 Ibid.
11 Ibid., 144–145.
12 Ibid.
13 Ibid., 145. *The Life of the Termites* had just been written in 1926; Maeterlinck had previously received the Nobel Prize for Literature in 1911.

peared Opa invented this review: 'At last a translation that brings something different from the original'");[14] my mother's teenage "crimes" (cutting classes at the *Gymnasium* with a note from her sweetheart, a "Dr. Stephan Kuttner," purportedly "the family physician").[15]

The Catholic interface begins upon the newly married couple's departure for Italy in 1933, where they were to live until 1940. We learn of her husband's interest in the historical roots of canon law, the developing high-level Vatican connections, the crucial job offer at Catholic University in Washington, D.C., the forthcoming American visa, the Vatican Passport for the entire family.[16] Tellingly, her own actual baptism just days before her wedding day, per the wishes of her husband-to-be, is not mentioned.[17] Indeed, the Catholic narrative is shockingly interrupted, in her telling, by my father's abrupt departure for Lisbon "to escape being put into a concentration Camp."[18] While Vatican officials play an indispensible if somewhat removed role in the plot, as does more immediately a generous, well-connected Italian "Callgirl," Pina,[19] the story my mother relates remains an overwhelmingly Jewish story about Jews, my family of Jews, desperately trying to escape certain death and, as she reminds us from the outset, not always successfully, as in the case of her deported grandmother.

I reproduce here in its entirety, divided into three segments, "the saga of my departure from Italy,"[20] occupying fully the last third of my mother's six-page single-spaced "kind of autobiography." To me, as to her many descendants to whom she so often narrated her story, what she calls her "saga" becomes the text's signal marker and overall significance, fixing as it does the inescapable (literally!) Jewishness at the heart of her narrative. The first segment[21] deals with her futile efforts to get out of Italy.

> This is a good moment in my story to tell you about the saga of my departure from Italy. When Dad left to go to Portugal he was issued a Vatican Passport for himself and also

---

14 App. I, 145.

15 Ibid., 145 – 146.

16 Ibid., 146. See pages 23 – 24 and below for a more complete and accurate account of the passport difficulties endured by the young family.

17 Ibid. My mother was to claim that she only converted to please my father and that she had no interest in religion, a stance that changed over the years as she began seeking emotional relief from various family problems in Catholic religious services.

18 Ibid.

19 Ibid., 147 – 148.

20 Ibid., 146.

21 Ibid., 146 – 147.

for me and our 3 children.[22] Susanne was exactly 6 weeks old. But I had been quite ill, the trip was a long one, by train, through Southern France and Spain, still not recovered from it's civil war and it seemed dangerous to expose us all to uncertain hardships; Dauling Hsü,[23] who at that time was Chargé d'Affaires in Italy, promised to get me out of Italy in case of an emergency "at worst, or best, as my wife No. 2." So we stayed. Then came this marvelous future in the U.S.[24] All I had to do was to get a transit Visa at the Portoguese Consulate, and a visa from the American Consulate. So, happily I went to the Portughese Cosulate, to be told, "show me the American Visa, and we will give you the Transit Visa." – on to the American Consulate to be told "show us your Portuguese Transit Visa and we will give you the American Visa. Tableau!!! This went on for weeks, beseeching the officials at the Portuguse place with letters from "important people," from De Gasperi to Cardinal Mercati[25]...to no avail. Practical me started selling our furniture, telling the individual buyers: I'll put the money you give me in a special account, – in case I do not succeed leaving you get your money back – and in case I can leave you get what you purchased after I will have left. –

What jumps out here? On the one hand, the intense, overwhelming danger ever looming; on the other, again the lightheartedness, the jokes. The humor of a well-placed, close family friend's mock bigamous offer offsetting an extremely serious situation: the father escaped to Lisbon, the young mother, quite ill, stranded with three small children, the youngest an infant. The endless futile shuttling between consulates, depicted as farce, "(Tableau!)." The impotence of the so-called "important people," De Gasperi, Mercati, at that time top-level officials in the Vatican hierarchy. My mother's indefatigable resourcefulness in a desperate situation, gathering cash in preparation for who knew what, refusing defeat.

---

22 My father left for Portugal at the end of May 1940. App. I, 146. On June 10, Italy entered the war, complicating both exit and entry visas for my mother.

23 Dauling Hsü was a close friend of my father's dating back from university days; he eventually returned to China, then on to Taiwan, and finally to Seattle, Washington. His family (his German wife, a close friend of my mother, and their three children) came to live with us in America in 1949, at which point our household language switched from German to English to help the new immigrant family.

24 A job offer at Catholic University in Washington D.C. arrived at the Vatican just two days after my father had fled to Portugal and was apparently transmitted to him there. App. I, 146.

25 A brief internet search reveals, variously, that Alcide De Gasperi was Prime Minister of Italy from 1945–1953, founder of the Christian Democratic Party, who presided over eight successive governments. Imprisoned in 1927 as a noted anti-fascist, upon his release he spent four years, from 1929–1943, in an administrative position at the Vatican Library. Cardinal Mercati had been a prefect at the Vatican Library and continued to hold many high-level appointments, including Archivist of the Vatican Secret Archives, from 1936 until 1957.

The second segment[26] brings us to the actual escape from Italy. The miraculous intervention of a high-class "Callgirl," Pina of flawless connections, a downstairs neighbor and friend, "the niece of so and so ... the chief of the Fascist Secret Police, the most feared man in all of Italy."[27]

> Now I have to go back a bit. In the apartment directly under ours lived a couple exactly our age, without children, I sometimes rode her bicycle, she sometimes borrowed our silverware, when she had dinnerguests. So, when she can came up and was interested in buying some things, I repeated my "conditions" of any sale. She asked "but, why don't you know whether you are really going to America?" and I told her of my problems. She then said "Well, I can help you to get the Port. Visa" "Why can you help me? I went there with letters from all those important people to no avail." She "don't you know who I am?" "Well you – you are are Pina" "Yes, but I also the niece of so and so . . the chief of the Fascist Secret Police, the most feared man in all of Italy!" She went on "Do you want me to take you to see Mussolini?" (it was like somebody asking me whether I would like to see the devil!) Pina was really like the character out of a novel, – she told me for example she would go to very rich people and say "I know you have, say, to pay 100.000,00 Dollars Income tax. I'll arrange it for you to have to pay only 70.000.00, you give me 10,000.00 so you save 20......." and did not add: or else. but beeng the niece of that man everybody did what she wanted Her uncle had no idea of all this: she also was a highly paid Callgirl, the famous dinnerparties enhanced by my silverware were given for her clients, among them one son of Mussolini. On the other hand she did not want a penny from me – or from the many jewish refugees she helped later on. A kind of Robin Hood mentality. – I got my Portuguese Transit Visa, She brought us to the Airprt (in the meantime, it was late in July, Italy had entered the war travel on land was not possible any more) my seat was taken in her name, so I had the best seat, opposite the American Ambassador, who flew to Madrid, in this small Plane, maybe for 20 passengers. And Susi got her first real compliment: On hearing that we were going to immigrate to the U.S. Ambassador Philips I think his name was said: "I am proud to be the first American to welcome such a beautiful little girl as a fellow citizen."

This second segment, with its amazing plot twists recounted in the same galloping prose, recounts how my mother and her children manage to get out of Italy through the miraculous intervention of a high class "Callgirl" with flawless connections, a downstairs neighbor and friend. My mother is forthright in expressing her outright revulsion at the Mussolini option, "(it was like somebody asking me whether I would like to see the devil!")". And yet Pina readily secures the all-important entry visa and drove them all to the airport, reserving my mother's seat in her own name, all because, in this telling, the two women connected through the womanly minutiae of their lives, borrowed silverware, shared bicy-

26 App. I, 147–148.
27 Ibid., 147.

cles, and the like. The warmth and mutual respect in the telling of this unlikely relationship shines through. In the end, it was my mother who knew "the important people," a woman's network after all.

The third segment[28] deals with the young family's increasingly desperate efforts to escape from Portugal. Almost reunited, yet maddeningly still separated by callous immigration officials—the scenario strikes an all too unpleasant contemporary resonance.

> Arriving in Lisbon, now as Eva Sarah Kuttner, with a big J in my German Passport, we were immediately herded into a special room – we could see Dad in the distance but were strictly forbidden to communicate with him – we had spent the previous night in the cellar airraid shelter, the British, on their way to France would drop leaflets over Rome, so the children had had maybe 3 hours of sleep and nothing to eat since dinner the night before (it was about 6 p.m. the following day, fortunately I was nursing Susanne.) There was not a word of complaint from the boys, even from my little "bad" Andrew; it seems children instinctly know when their parents are powerless, When I complained I was told sternly to behave myself, they were considering to send us to Germany – 2 Nazi types, obviously Germans, were standing nearby – how I longed for my Grandmother's suicide pills [heavily scratched out] – Dad had disappeared – to return about an hour later (the then airport was close to the City) with an official of the Apostolic Delegation and his Vatican Passport with all of us on it – we were important people and FREE TO GO

And so we arrive at the harrowing scene in the Lisbon airport, my mother's German passport, marked with a giant **J** and a new, Nazi-imposed name, Sarah,[29] no other passport in hand, she and her children detained despite Portugal's supposed neutrality, openly threatened with deportation to Germany and certain death. Again, the mention of suicide pills, heavily scratched out in the original text, a rejected alternative like her grandmother's later one was to be.[30] Does her attempted redaction reflect her effort to protect us from the horror of her final desperation? Mother and children are finally released through a last Vatican intervention, my mother claims, a claim strongly contested by my father's interview late in life, some ten years prior to the "sort of autobiography."[31] He relates

---

28 App. I, 148.
29 Under Nazi decrees of 1938 and 1939, Jews without "specified" Jewish names had to adopt an additional first name, "Israel" for men and "Sarah" for women. See Thomas S. Kuttner, "Stephan Kuttner: Both German Jew and Catholic Scholar," *Journal of Law, Philosophy and Culture* 5, no. 1 (2010): 47, note 15.
30 See App. I, 148. Times cross here: how could she know about grandmother's 1941 suicide pills in 1940? Writing in 1998, logic and time apparently fade in the urgency of her recollections.
31 See Thomas S. Kuttner, 47–48, drawing on interviews he conducted with his father in 1988. For a well-researched account on the controversial Vatican response to raging antisemitism, see

a markedly different story of local Apostolic Delegate indifference and worse, reflecting internal Vatican tensions. In his telling, when he frantically tried to contact the Apostolic Nuncio (as the official Vatican representative in Portugal was called) for help, he was told that the official was at dinner and could not be disturbed. Desperately resourceful, he then telephoned a young Portuguese police officer whom he had befriended during his brief sojourn in Lisbon. The young officer, who must have had some sort of official role in immigration matters, immediately arranged for my mother's detention to be lifted. [32] Once again, as in my mother's story, high officialdom having failed, it was the compassion of chance acquaintances, ordinary people, perhaps Fascist Party members even, that made all the difference. Finally, "important people" themselves, armed with a Vatican passport and a job offer in America, the reunited family was "FREE TO GO," my mother proclaims in a last jubilant note.[33]

And here, abruptly, my mother's "sort of autobiography" ends. Nothing of the intervening nearly sixty years, the birth of six more children, the new life in America, the early impoverished years as refugees, the later more affluent ones as my father's career took him to ever more prestigious (and well-paying) institutions. Did my mother, then aged 84, simply just run out of steam at this point? (She was to live another nine years.) To the contrary, I would say. In my view, she had completed the task she had set out to do. Her narrative was complete. She had told us "your family history." This was her autobiography, the ultimate significance of her life. She has made sure that her story, her legacy, is preserved. Her escape story and its backdrop, told and retold so often to her children and grandchildren in our own personal Haggadah, the details varying perhaps but the sharp outlines never softened, were now memorialized in a final archival form. Memory preserved as story-telling, story-telling preserved as text, persistent sources of Jewish identity from its very beginnings, resurface here in my mother's tale of a hybrid Jewish identity triumphantly emerging from the chaos and madness of history. The familiar tropes of persecution, flight, and rebirth, underscored by God's miraculous intervention (the prostitute! the police officer! modern *doppelganger* to the Torah's mysterious *Ish*/messengers?) emerge again in a new Exodus, no doubt unconsciously reprised in my mother's narra-

Susan Zuccotti, *Under his Very Windows: The Vatican and the Holocaust in Italy* (New Haven: Yale University Press, 2002). For a detailed accounting of my father's relationship to the Vatican during the years 1938–1940, see Ludwig Schmugge, "Stephan Kuttner (1907–1996) the 'Pope' of Canon Law Studies Between Germany, the Vatican and the USA," trans. Michael Kuttner, *Bulletin of Medieval Canon Law*, vol. 30 (2013), 141–165, 154–161. See also Chapter 2 below, pages 36–37.
32 Thomas S. Kuttner, 47–48.
33 App. I, 148.

tive, and serve as key markers of the persistence of Jewish identity in conversion. What my mother, never by choice a writer as the physical manuscript, reproduced in part above, abundantly makes clear, nonetheless apparently felt compelled to painfully commit to writing near the end of her long life was her own personal act of *zakhor*. In it, her rich recollection of a lost German Jewish world becomes a highly personal and intercultural narrative of a Jewish identity under stress. *Writing the Jewish self*, writing history.

Aftershocks

And so my mother sank into the life in America that my father had ordained for her, the world of priests and bishops, his Catholic students, colleagues and friends, the world of prohibited birth control, baptisms for all the new babies that inevitably followed, the world of weekly church attendance, Catholic school education for the children, first communions, nuns. So what became of the world of the Eva Sarah Kuttner, her passport marked with a J? Leaving aside, for the moment, her almost obsessive telling and retelling of her Nazi escape story to each and every one of her nine children and eighteen grandchildren, stories burned into their collective consciousness as their own stories will attest, key moments stand out in stark relief.

Most striking, in my mind, is the sort of rite of passage instruction of our adolescence. Did each of us receive the same instruction? Apparently so, per my recent informal survey. I remember mine vividly. At some point in my early adolescence, at the age of thirteen or fourteen perhaps, me a student in a private Catholic girls' high school, my mother took me aside. This was a striking event in itself; there were very few truly private conversations in our crowded household. In a markedly serious, hushed tone she said to me, as I recall it: *You are getting older now. Someday you will fall in love and perhaps want to marry. When this happens, you must tell the person you love that you are a Jew. He might not want to marry you.* What rang in my ears the most at the time (marriage seemed very far off to me!) was the harsh, almost scolding voice she used to deliver this incredibly startling pronouncement. *You are a Jew.* She had never before directly said that to me, never before called me a Jew, and she did so now with a force and a clarity that I would never forget.

Cynthia Baker, in her recent brilliant treatise on the word *Jew*, the word italicized throughout,[34] reminds us of the violence that the word *Jew*, historically

---

34 Baker, xiii.

imposed from without, she insists, and always signifier of the absolute (and inferior) Other, has engendered.[35] That violence begins, she argues, in the psyche, the very naming of *Jew* received as a blow, struck from without.[36] As an example, she brings us to Derrida's recollections of his own naming as a Jew, in a passage well worth repeating.

> Before understanding any of it, I received this word like a blow, a denunciatio, a de-legitimation prior to any right, prior to any legality. A blow struck [*un coup porté*] against me, but a blow that I would henceforth have to carry and incorporate [*porter, comporter*] forever in the very essence of my most singularly signed and assigned ... *comportment* ... .[...] This word, this performative address ... this apostrophe was, remains, and carries, older than the claim [*constat*], more archaic than any constative, the figure of a wounding arrow, of a weapon or projectile that has sunk into your body, once and for all and without the possibility of ever uprooting it. It adheres to your body and pulls it toward itself from within ...[37]

Baker also recalls for us the figure of Rahel Varnhagen, introduced to us earlier. Almost two decades before her 1814 conversion, Rahel was to write:

> I have this strange fancy: it is as if some supramundane being, just as I was thrust into this world, plunged these words with a dagger into my heart: [...] 'Be a Jewess!' And now my life is a slow bleeding to death.[38]

Naomi Seidman, in recent remarks on Baker's work,[39] provocatively raises the possibility of a parallel violence imposed by the word *Jew* from within, doubling Derrida's shocking image of the "wounding arrow" from without with the intrafamilial violent inscription of circumcision from within, which serves the double

---

35 "For most of two long millennia, the word *Jew* has been predominantly defined and delimited as a term for the *not-self*. It has often signified an absolute *other*, the very antithesis of the Western Christian *self*." Baker, 4; see generally ibid., 3–8.
36 Ibid., 47–49.
37 Ibid., 48–49. Italics in Baker. See Jacques Derrida, *Judeities: Questions for Jacques Derrida*, eds. Bettina Bergo, Joseph Coohen, and Raphael Zagury-Orley, trans. Bettina Bergo and Michael B. Smith (New York: Fordham University Press, 2007), 10–11. Baker also references for us Kafka's perception of the word *"Jew"* as a "blow, flying unerringly forward," in a remark to Milena Jesenská. Baker, 48, citing to Franz Kafka, *Letters to Malena*, trans. Phillip Boehm (New York: Schocken Books, 1990), 46.
38 See Baker, note 5, 158–159.
39 Naomi Seidman, "Jewish Identity as a Psychic Wound," *Marginalia Review of Books* June 19, 2017, https://marginalia.lareviewofbooks.org/jewish-identity-psychic-wound/. Discussing Baker's project, among others, Seidman proposes that "Jewishness (or consciousness of Jewishness), at least for Kafka, Derrida, and other Jewish moderns, begins as a trauma, and that *Jew* is an imposition on a consciousness and self that both precedes and exceeds it." Seidman, 2.

purpose of striking the blow of gender as well. Varnhagen's anguished plaint, then, applying Seidman's striking insight, gains additional coherence as an act of parallel circumcision, gendered violence bloodily imposed by the very act of birth itself, "the slow bleeding to death" of the command, "Be a Jewess!," the "slow bleeding" also an obvious marker of gender, of menstruation. "So can we really separate the violence that is gender from the violence that is the *Jew?*" Seidman asks.[40]

And so my mother called me out, engraving me, inscribing me specifically, personally, unforgettably, with the word Jew. Here, of course, the naming, my naming as a Jew, falls within the Seidman analysis, a blow struck from within, and specifically within a gendered context, that of an presumed heterosexual marriage. Is it too great a stretch to find in this moment, within the odd liminal world inhabited by my family, an echo of the quintessential bar/bat mitzvah moment, the moment when we were called upon to be adults, to take on the burden of Jewishness in all its limitations and disabilities? Limits that Rahel Varnhagen, at the dawn of modernity, experienced all too clearly? It definitely was our moment of truth, our awakening to the real world.

But what did it mean, then, to be a Jew? My mother was unable to provide much more. Raised in her own wholly secular, thoroughly assimilated, affluent German Jewish milieu, severed from all connection to a Jewish tradition, a Jewish practice, my mother's overwhelming experience of Jewishness was that of assault. And it was as an assault that she passed it on to me, to us. Years later, my brother Philip offered a different interpretation. "Mom said the same thing to me, with gender reversal. I think she was trying to protect us." Another brother, Michael, also remembers the moment as a protective gesture (and one that implicitly inferred a gentile union). I would phrase it a little differently. I would say that she was trying to warn us, a warning stemming from her own hidden pain. Warn us of the possibility, inevitability even, of an ever-looming assault, a blow. Warn us that we were and would always be Jews, the Other. And how prescient indeed, in today's post-Charlottesville era in my country of birth. I can only be grateful that my mother did not live to see it.

And yet withal, my mother also instilled in us the meaning of *Jew*, of Jewishness, as a moment of secret pride. How special we were, how tied to the great cultural heroes of the world of *Bildung* so revered by my parents and by German Jews in general, a mark of distinction that set them apart for over one hundred and fifty years.[41] How frequently my mother would remind us of her own moth-

---

40 Seidman, "Jewish Identity," 3
41 See generally, Mendes-Flohr and Mosse.

er's acclaimed translations of Maeterlinck, and of her mother-in-law's musical bent as a violinist and regular member of a string quarter that included the soon to be world-famous Albert Einstein's mother. A Jewish world of *Bildung* presided over by women, passed on by women.[42] In one memorable instance, in the summer of 1967, my mother took those of us who happened to be in Europe at the time (four younger brothers, myself, my father) to see a Jewish cemetery near the village of Schopfloch in Bavaria, its neglected gravestones miraculously preserved.[43] Pointing out the Hebrew inscriptions, she told us with pride, *your ancestors were rabbis.* (Male ancestors of course.) Was this the first time I had heard this? All I know is that this particular outing, and above all the Hebrew inscriptions on the gravestones, the script I had never before encountered, the script of my ancestors! – all this left a huge impression on me.

But a darker narrative invariably predominated. Certain incidents spring to mind. For instance. In the late sixties my mother reluctantly came to support the antiwar movement, her reservations stemming from her fierce pride in her adopted American citizenship alongside her fierce sense of loyalty to the country that had taken in her and her young family. And yet, what stands out so forcefully for me about her reaction to the events of that time was the bitter comment she made to me one day. *When I was young, they hated me because I was a Jew. Now they hate me because I am old.* So much secretly carried pain, triggered by yet another mass movement, new scenes of street violence, new huge parades, her fear of the mob reignited. I've never forgotten that moment.

There were other examples. As my interest in my family's Judaism deepened, I once naively asked my mother whether she had heard about *Kristallnacht* when living in Rome in 1938. She responded in a blast of terrible anger, of outrage, of pain. *Of course I heard about it. How can you even ask me that? It was a terrible, terrible thing* ("*furchtbar, furchtbar!*"). I quickly backed off, as I clearly was meant to do. In another moment of naiveté, one day I urged my mother to see *The Garden of the Finzi-Continis,* the wonderful 1970 movie by Vittorio de Sica. An acknowledged masterpiece, the film traces the fate of an extremely wealthy Italian Jewish family inexorably dragged into the maelstrom of Italian fascism, unprotected by their fine clothes, their private tennis lessons, their whole luxurious

---

42 As background, see Marion A. Kaplan, *The Making of the Jewish Middle Class.* (Oxford: Oxford University Press, 1991) for the changing role of Jewish women in Imperial Germany.

43 A brief internet search under the heading "Schopfloch Jewish Cemetery" yields multiple images and links to newspaper articles detailing the several websites devoted to this site. The cemetery dates from 1632 to 1937 and unaccountably was not destroyed by the Nazis, although none of the town's Jewish inhabitants survived the *Shoah.* My maternal grandfather's family came from Schopfloch, although his immediate family had moved to Paris before he was born in 1872.

way of life, increasingly isolated within the walls of their stunningly beautiful estate. To me, the first American-born child of my family, acutely aware of the material scarcity that permeated our early refugee days, the film offered a window into a lost world, the world of the proud, affluent, western European Jew and its fateful trajectory. Again seeking understanding, I sought to draw from her a parallel to her own less wealthy but nonetheless unmistakably prosperous seemingly carefree family life in Berlin and its gradual erosion and final ending. Apparently succumbing to my urging to see the film, my beloved mother shortly thereafter again erupted in a furious tirade against me. *How could you send me to see this terrible movie. How could you be so cruel!* Another moment of painful bewilderment for me, as, seeking to go beyond the silence, seeking to understand, I caught a glimpse of the shock of a life shattered by history.

Like so many survivors, my mother wanted to, almost had to, I would say, control the narrative. The story of her family and the Nazis was hers to tell, she seemed to insist, to tell in her own inimitable *Berliner* style, rich in sly irony, humor and pathos, a promised land always in sight. That story, "written to amuse you all," we heard over and over. Beyond that we were forbidden to go. And yet at every turn a darker truth leaked out. *You are Jewish. Own it, claim it. But be warned, bad things, terrible things, can come of it.* Judaism experienced as a blow, the ultimate blow even, coming from outside. As noted, Naomi Seidman has alerted us to the blow of Judaism likewise coming from within, within the family. I would say that the Judaism with which we were all inscribed, enrolled in even, was a dual and gendered blow as my mother stubbornly insisted on connecting us with our heritage. Her tales operated as a simultaneously imposed trauma of naming both from without and within, so at odds with the Catholic world we supposedly inhabited. And this was how we were named, how I was named, both in her oft-repeated escape tale and even more sharply in her rare, uncensored, blurted-out remarks. Indeed, I would argue that surely my mother's family origin story, preserved as archive in her old age, endlessly repeated to each and every one of her nine children and eighteen grandchildren over a long lifetime in a family in which almost all specifically Jewish content had been lost, operated to strike the blow simultaneously from without and within for us all.

Final Moments

As my father's health began to decline, my mother began to express a much more open interest in Jewish themes and a Jewish fate. To my surprise, in the early nineties she asked me to take her to an exhibit of children's art from Theresienstadt at the University of California's Berkeley Art Museum. By this time she was no longer driving, her vision beginning to fail. So off we went, she peering at length at every single drawing, reminding me from time to time (as if I needed a reminder!) that her grandmother had been murdered there. She always spat out the word "murdered" like a curse.[44] As mentioned earlier, her photo was ever present. How thrilled my mother was when I told her that I had enrolled her grandmother's name, Dora Ullman, in the archives of the Holocaust Memorial Museum in Washington, D.C.

Later still, in 2003, increasingly frail, my mother asked me to take her to a Chagall exhibit at the San Francisco Museum of Modern Art. By this time, her energy and her eyesight were seriously compromised, yet once again she painstakingly examined each and every piece, murmuring to me from time to time, *Chagall was a Jew, you know*. She lingered for a long time over Chagall's controversial, *"White Crucifixion."*[45] The painting depicts a crucifixion embedded in numerous iconic Jewish symbols interwoven with brutal scenes of persecution. The duality of the central figure of Jesus on the cross is emphasized: his loin cloth a *tallit* with its black stripes and fringes, his head covered with some sort of ritual cloth instead of a crown of thorns, above the cross the traditional Christian inscription INRI (Jesus of Nazareth King of the Jews) doubled in Aramaic, *Yeshu HaNotzre Malcha D'Yejudai,* the halo surrounding the head doubled by a haloed menorah at the feet. The striking central image is surrounded by many equally striking images of Jewish persecution: on the right, a synagogue ark in flames, its torah scroll exposed, ritual objects flung about, a soldier overseeing the destruction,[46] below a fleeing Jew, a bulging, lumpy bag on his back, could these be more ritual objects stuffed within? To the left, more scenes: another man in flight, clutching a Torah scroll and gazing backwards in horror, and yet anoth-

---

44 Years later, she gave the exhibit catalog to her grandchild (and my niece) Michele as a gift for her fortieth birthday, insistently inscribed "Your great-great-grandmother died in October 1941 in Terezin."

45 1938: Art Institute of Chicago. An image of this painting is available at: https://www.artic.edu/artworks/59426/white-crucifixion.

46 Earlier configurations and sketches show a reversed swastika on the flag above the burning ark and on the soldier's armband. See Ziva Amishai-Maisels, "Chagall's 'White Crucifixion,'"*Art Institute of Chicago Museum Studies* 17, no. 2 (1991): 139–81, 140–143. doi:10.2307/4101588. Amishai-Maisels concludes that these details, as well as the painting's dating by the artist as 1938, clearly link the painting to the period's Nazi atrocities in Germany, including Kristallnacht, and may have been obscured by the artist to protect the painting, first exhibited in Paris in 1940 shortly before the Nazi invasion of France. Ibid., 140. Oddly enough, in my recollection the Nazi symbols were clearly visible.

er man wearing a prominent, indecipherably lettered sign.[47] Above, still more scenes of desperation: an overcrowded unseaworthy craft, stuffed with refugees, a burning village reduced to ruins, complete with corpse, soldiers sharing the spoils, a group of what appear to be Red Army partisans approaching, to help or to hurt. With the exception of the soldiers and the ambiguous partisans, all of the figures read as *Ostjuden*, in keeping with the rest of the artist's body of work. Crowning the painting, the flying figures of four Jewish angels or patriarchs, most clearly perhaps a Moses and a Rachel, are bewailing the suffering below.[48]

Ziva Amishai-Maisel, an Israeli art historian, reminding us of the enormous controversy engendered by the problematic nature of the work,[49] situates the *White Crucifixion* and its treatment of Jesus as crucified Jew within the context of Chagall's other similarly themed works as well as within a Jewish Christological tradition, primarily Russian, in which Jesus serves as stand-in for all persecuted Jewish victims.[50] Here in the *White Crucifixion*, as in his other crucifixion pieces of the period, Chagall is clearly reacting to and commenting on the cruel events of his times.[51] Indeed, a recent biographer claims, "one monumental canvas—*White Crucifixion*— ... stood out to become, like Picasso's *Guernica*, Chagall's masterpiece and major political statement of the late 1930s."[52] And yet unlike his iconic, mystical, even joyful evocations of the lost Hasidic world of his childhood, Chagall's crucifixion paintings point to a troublingly unresolved engagement of this enormously famous, non-practicing Jewish artist with his Jewish past. Towards the end of his life, he created monumental stained glass windows for both Jewish and Christian sites, notably for the Hebrew University's Hadassah Medical Center ("the "Jerusalem Windows"), for cathedrals in Metz (1968) and in Reims (1974), and for St. Stephen's Church in Mainz (1978), among others. Chagall was to be buried in 1985 in a Christian cemetery in the south of France, with only a stranger stepping forward to say Kaddish.[53]

And what was my mother thinking there, at the San Francisco Museum of Modern Art, in 2003? I would say that for my mother, whom we left lingering in front of Chagall's *White Crucifixion*, the painting fascinated her enormously because it somehow embodied the ambivalences, conflicts, and contradictions

---

47 In the original version, the sign read "Ich bin Jude."
48 I am grateful to Amishai-Maisels for the identifications.
49 See Amishai-Maisels, 139 and 180, note 1.
50 Ibid., 143–153.
51 See ibid., 142.
52 Jackie Wullschläger, *Chagall* (New York, Alfred A. Knopf, 2008), 378.
53 Ibid., 522.

of her own life experience as a converted Jew and a Jewish identity that she was unable and unwilling to abandon.

We drove back in silence, a companionable one it seemed, to her Berkeley apartment where she now lived alone, already a widow for seven years. I end my meditation here with this last glimpse of my frail elderly mother, a profoundly private person despite her strong outgoing personality, still exploring the deeply felt mysteries, the unresolved ambiguities of her life, able for a moment to hold them within their frame, the frame of the painting, the frame of her own life, at peace, it seemed, at last.

2 My Father: In Search Of The Hidden Jew

Was du ererbt von deinen Vätern hast,
Erwirb es, um es zu besitzen.

What you inherit from your fathers,
Earn it, in order to possess it.

– Johann Wolfgang von Goethe,
Faust: Der Tragödie, Erster Teil[1]

I had eyelid surgery shortly before beginning work on this chapter. As a result, my eyes are considerably larger than they had been for quite awhile. Indeed, I startle every morning at the mirror. Gazing out at me I see my father's eyes. Fitting indeed, I say, as I begin this part of my book. My father's eyes, searching for my father.

How difficult it is for me to write about my father, Stephan Kuttner, his public self so well known, his private one so well hidden, the man who so often chose to be absent from our boisterous family scene. Unlike my mother, he left few clues about his Jewish self. And no wonder, for his own birth family had become "officially" Lutheran in the wake of the conversion of his own father, Georg Kuttner, sometime around the turn of the twentieth century in what was no doubt a career move.[2] Georg Kuttner's three children were baptized in the state religion as they arrived, beginning with the eldest in 1905; his wife Gertrude Schocken Kuttner remained Jewish, albeit non-observant. How these religious displacements and dynamics played out within the family remain unknown. There were other instances of baptisms in the extended Kuttner-Schocken families; most, however, retained the largely secular Jewish identities of their class and era. We do know about Georg Kuttner's violent suicide in 1916 (he threw himself under a train), leaving behind a wife and three young children. My father, the second child and only boy, was nine. According to my mother, the storyteller, the children were informed of his death not by their mother but by the maid; Georg Kuttner's name was never again uttered in the house, she said. My mother tells this particular tale in hushed, even secretive tones. My father never spoke of his childhood. We are left only, belatedly, with a sepia portrait, dated 1918, of three beautiful, dark-haired, dark-eyed children.

---

1 Translation by Michael P. Steinberg in *Judaism Musical and Unmusical* (Chicago: University of Chicago Press, 2007), 22.
2 Georg Kuttner's career in law embraced both an academic and a judicial track. A record of his baptism, which probably occurred shortly before his marriage in 1903 or 1904, remains elusive.

https://doi.org/10.1515/9783110731965-007

We move forward to the adult Stephan Kuttner and his meteoric rise to international academic acclaim as the world's foremost scholar in the rarefied world of medieval canon law. His academic and professional trajectory begins in the midst of the Nazi rise to power in Berlin and in Rome, continues in a refugee's America in the relatively obscure academic backwaters of the Catholic University of America in Washington, D.C., and culminates eventually in endowed chairs at Yale University and later at the University of California in Berkeley. Along the way, numerous honorary degrees and prestigious honors are amassed at home and abroad, among them, most notably, membership in the l'Institut de France and later, the award of the Pour le Mérite, Germany's highest civilian honor.[3]

Stephan Kuttner's Jewishness is veiled in most official sources. At most, it is referred to almost glancingly as "of Jewish ancestry" or "of Jewish descent." Indeed, his *New York Times* obituary of August 16, 1996 omits any reference to his Jewishness. Perhaps that is what my father would have preferred.

Early along the way, Stephan Kuttner abandoned what appeared to be at most a rather lackluster Lutheranism, his last contact being a pro forma confirmation as a boy of perhaps fourteen.[4] The family did not attend church; instruction in the state religion was part of the school curriculum.[5] Later we see a young man's growing interest in Roman Catholicism, arising out of what began as a purely academic inquiry during his postdoctoral research to become what appears to have been, unlike his father's, a conversion of conviction. As he tells it some sixty years later, his initial interest in the origin and development of certain aspects of criminal law (his recently completed doctoral dissertation was on the law of perjury) led him to the study of the history of canon law,[6] at that time a

---

3 My father died in 1996. An internet search brings up several official and unofficial obituaries detailing highlights of his professional career. His extensive papers are now on deposit at Yale University in the collection known as the Stephan Kuttner Institute of Medieval Canon Law.

4 Stephan Kuttner, interview by Thomas Kuttner, Berkeley, California, February-March 1988, unedited transcript, 162; henceforth, Stephan Kuttner Interview. The interview tapes, recorded over four days in February and March 1988, and their transcriptions are likewise housed in the Stephan Kuttner Institute of Medieval Canon Law, Yale University. See also Thomas S. Kuttner, "Stephan Kuttner: Both German Jew and Catholic Scholar," 43 – 65.

5 Stephan Kuttner Interview, 162. My father reports that his never-converted mother told him that he was Jewish around the twelve years of age when he reported antisemitic incidents at school. Ibid., 160 – 161. Again, Derrida's "blow," struck from without in a somewhat parallel schoolboy experience to Derrida's and from within, per Seidman, by his mother. The interview transcript remains silent as to my father's reaction.

6 The term 'canon law' refers to the religious and civil law of the Roman Catholic Church, dating back in its various forms to the Church's earliest days. It is now well established that canon law exercised a broad influence on the development of modern civil and common law across Western Europe.

purely secular subject in German law schools. In 1930, at age twenty-six, he left for Rome to do research for his *Habilitation*[7] at the Vatican Library. The trajectory that took him into the heart of Roman Catholicism, triggered by his legal interests, was to become intensely personal in the wake of a quasi-mystical experience in an ancient Roman basilica that year in an eerie counterpoint, as I see it, to Franz Rosenzweig's more famous *Ich bleibe also Jüdisch* some seventeen years earlier.[8] Like Rosenzweig, my father too was searching for religious meaning, in his case, in the hauntingly beautiful old churches of Rome. As he explains his conversion some fifty years later, "Partly it was the atmosphere – but partly it was an interior act – of wanting to believe. ... Sitting in a church, especially in one of the very old Roman basilicas in Rome, would bring me closer to a Catholic feeling."[9]

As such, I see my father as a late arrival to some of the preoccupations of the Weimar era (1918–1933), known, among other things, as a period of intense religious questioning among both Jews and Christians as traditional religious and social beliefs fell away in the wake of the disastrous defeat of World War I.[10] For the young Martin Buber (1878–1965), the inclusion of a Jewish-Christian dialogue was an essential component of the Jewish Renaissance; indeed, the Jewish-Christian encounter became a recurrent theme in the pages of *Der Jude*, the political and literary journal he founded in 1916.[11] We know from the story of Franz Rosenzweig, co-founder with Buber of the *Freies Jüdisches Lehrhaus* in Frankfurt in 1920, that mixed Jewish-Christian convert families in the professionalized Jewish bourgeoisie, like my father's family, were not uncommon.[12] Indeed, the youthful Rosenzweig was deeply involved in religious debate

---

7 In the German university system, while the completion of a doctoral degree could lead to an unpaid teaching position, the post-doctoral *Habilitation* or full-length book was a prerequisite for an actual academic appointment.

8 On the eve of his anticipated conversion to Christianity, Franz Rosenzweig's conviction that he had to convert "qua Jew" led him to re-engage with his heritage. Three months later, attending a Yom Kippur service in a small orthodox synagogue, he apparently experienced an overwhelming spiritual moment that led him to embrace the passionate Judaism that transformed his life and his work. See Nahum N. Glatzer, *Franz Rosenzweig: His Life and Thought* (New York: Farrar, Straus and Young, 1953) 24–28.

9 Stephan Kuttner Interview, 168: for context see, generally, 167–169.

10 See David N. Myers, *Resisting History* (Oxford, Princeton: Princeton University Press, 2003), 69–70.

11 See Paul Mendes-Flohr, *Divided Passions: Jewish Intellectuals and the Experience of Modernity* (Detroit: Wayne State University Press, 1990), 133–167 for a thorough discussion of the German Jewish-Christian encounter of the period.

12 See Myers, 75–77.

with both Hans and Rudolf Ehrenberg, his soon-to-convert cousins, and with Eugen Rosenstock-Huessy, already a convert, whose passionate embrace of an experiential, quasi-ecstatic Christianity profoundly influenced Rosenzweig's development before and after his embrace of a fully lived Judaism.[13]

Historically, waves of conversions (*Taufepidemie*) were a recurrent phenomenon among the Jewish upper classes throughout the nineteenth century and, to a lesser extent, into the twentieth.[14] Indeed, within the contemporary musical world that had so fascinated my father (a serious music student and sometime composer throughout his youth and thereafter),[15] significant figures, among them, Gustav Mahler, Arthur Schoenberg, Bruno Walter, and Otto Klemperer, had converted to Christianity.

My father's trajectory, however, was notably different from that of a Buber or a Rosenzweig (or, for that matter, his modern musical heroes). Already largely separated from a Judaism he scarcely knew, in the grip of an intellectual and spiritual passion that would dominate the rest of his life, he decisively embraced baptism in the Roman Catholic faith just days before his August 1933 wedding in Berlin, bringing my mother along. The newlywed couple departed the next day for Rome and my father's research position at the Vatican Library, obtained through the intervention of one of his Catholic mentors. The first year, ironically, was financed by a branch of the German government, even though as a "full Jew" his academic and juridical path forward in Germany had already been barred by racial regulations promulgated as emergency measures shortly after Hitler's appointment as Chancellor.[16] In Rome, my father managed for a time to find a measure of protection, along with other Jewish converts, as an employee of the Vatican, then as now a sovereign state, despite surveillance measures initiated by the German embassy in Rome. By 1938, in a rapidly darkening Europe, newly enacted Italian Fascist laws put him under threat of immediate in-

---

13 Myers, 81–84; Glatzer, 24–28. Their youthful, extended, serious discussions on the nature and relationship of Christianity and Judaism are memorialized in a remarkable series of letters from 1916. See *Judaism Despite Christianity*, ed. Eugen Rosenstock-Huessy (New York: Schocken Books, 1971.)

14 Briefly described in my Introduction. Readers interested in a more detailed presentation are encouraged to consult Botelho, "Modern Marranism," 6–20.

15 Stephan Kuttner Interview, 1–24.

16 The Enabling Act, granting Hitler extraordinary powers to rule by decree, was passed by the Reichstag on March 24, 1933. The Law for the Restoration of the Professional Civil Service (*Gesetz zur Wiederherstellung des Berufsbeamtentums*), passed on April 7, 1933, decreeing that "Civil servants who are not of Aryan descent are to be retired." See Saul Friedländer, *Nazi German and the Jews*, vol. 1, *The Years of Persecution* (New York: HarperCollins Publisher, 1997), 17, 27; Thomas S. Kuttner, 44, note 2.

carceration and deportation. My father's urgent request to the Vatican for a diplomatic passport that would have provided full diplomatic immunity for himself and his family, hence freedom to travel, was turned down in favor of a "special" passport that provided little to no protection.[17] His German passport, of course, marking him as a Jew, left him subject to the full measure of increasingly restrictive Italian and German racial laws. By June 1940, Italy had entered the war alongside Germany and established its own concentration camps. A side effect was that the visa arrangements that permitted my father to travel to Portugal two months earlier were nullified. My mother's escape narrative, the center of the preceding chapter, dominates the rest of the family story.

As set forth earlier in my Introduction, Todd Endelman uses the phrase "radical assimilation" to describe the well-documented wave of conversions among nineteenth-century German Jews. Most recently, in his ambitious 2015 book, *Leaving the Jewish Fold*, Endelman significantly enlarges his purview in both time and space to broadly survey the phenomenon of Jewish conversion from early medieval to postmodern times across a pan-European, British, and North American landscape.[18] For the modern period, Endelman statistically explores conversion by levels of acculturation, integration, and secularization, as well as by occupation, social rank, and economic status.[19] His inescapable conclusion is that most if not all Jewish conversions in this period remained basically opportunistic, or, to use a gentler term, pragmatic.[20] More controversially, Endelman ultimately proposes that his study of Jewish conversion reveals the limitations of the entire European emancipation project.[21]

---

17 I am extremely grateful to Ludwig Schmugge for a detailed accounting of my father's convoluted relationship with the Vatican in the period between 1938 and 1940, a relationship that included Vatican officials' surveillance reports on "Jewish foreigners," among them my father, to the German embassy. Schmugge, 154–161.

18 Endelman, *Leaving the Jewish Fold*. Endelman distinguishes the term "radical assimilation," "an umbrella term," from "conversion," "the religious act of formally embracing Christianity." Ibid., 16.

19 Thus, Endelman specifies, the majority of conversions occurred not in the world of commerce, but in civil service, law, science, the arts, academia, and the media. Ibid., 125–126. A breakdown by gender is included only minimally and rather dismissively. See e. g. ibid., 122–123, which provides examples of Jewish women's pre-marriage conversions, described dismissively as "erotic attachment." My mother's conversion could perhaps be implicated within this rubric.

20 Ibid., 118–119.

21 Ibid., 360–367. Indeed, I would argue that Endelman ultimately rejects what he calls the Jewish embrace of modernity; instead, despite his disclaimers, I see him adopting the proto-Zionist claim that Jewish life in the diaspora is doomed. Ibid., 365–366. I would of course disagree with this assessment, as the thrust of this monograph makes clear.

To me the thrust of Endelman's research is probably more characteristic of the initial Kuttner family move, that of Georg Kuttner, my paternal grandfather, into the state religion as a way of academic and professional advancement. Indeed, as Endelman spells out in telling statistical detail, barriers for Jews seeking careers in academia and in the judiciary were stringent during the years of my paternal grandfather's career at the turn of the twentieth century.[22] The son, however, was already one radical step removed, to use Endelman's terminology, from a Jewish identity; indeed, he seems to have been in revolt against a northern European Protestantism as well. As a young adult, he reports, he was repulsed by Lutheranism, finding in it a "nationalistic, *völkisch* spirit that existed in the Lutheran church, and I found so many traits of that in Luther himself."[23] In its place, he gravitated towards a southern European Catholicism, eventually finding a sort of haven there.[24] His certainly was not, as some detractors have urged, an opportunistic conversion to avoid or escape the manifold dangers in 1930s Germany of his indisputable Jewish ancestry. My father, after all, had spent years as a student of criminal and constitutional law and wrote his Ph.D. dissertation on the theory of perjury in criminal law, which was to lead him, in preparing for his *Habilitation*, into the world of canon law. Indeed, already part of a low-level judicial apparatus, he had experienced by early 1933 the implications of the administrative regulations that preceded the 1935 Nuremberg laws. Forbidden to proceed with his *Habilitation* at the university, he also was asked to resign his civil service position of law clerk; indignantly, he claims, he refused to resign and insisted on being dismissed.[25] A whole cohort of civil servants and academics went with him, as he vividly remembers, in the first gutting of the university's faculty and graduate student body after Hitler's election in February 1933.[26] To him and to his generation, "this was a prelude to legitimating legislation."[27] After all, as he well understood, my father had four Jewish grandparents, a Jewish mother, a Jewish convert father, Jewish aunts, uncles and cousins, and other relatives more removed. The implications could not fail to be glaringly apparent to him.

---

22 Endelman, 103–104.
23 Stephan Kuttner Interview, 168.
24 Steinberg differentiates between German and Austrian Judaism, which he places along a north-south axis mapping the majority Protestant-Catholic culture. Steinberg, *Judaism Musical and Unmusical*, 23. It is interesting in this context that my father went south to embrace a new faith.
25 Stephan Kuttner Interview, 130.
26 Ibid., 131. "My reaction was, turn your back on Germany." Ibid., 132.
27 Ibid., 128.

My father remained throughout his life a complex man, the various threads of his personal identity kept close. The ambiguities abound. His students and colleagues early in his teaching career at the Catholic University of America in Washington, D.C. were priests, many destined to became bishops and beyond. The Roman Catholic clergy, and particularly its hierarchy, remained well within his personal and professional comfort zone throughout his later years, along with lay academic colleagues of course, yet he was indisputably a family man, however distant, the father of nine. His Jewish identity remained closely guarded, though never denied; when pressed, he spoke of Jewish "ancestry." Few knew of his ultimately futile, desperate efforts to free his father-in-law's sister who was to also eventually die at Theresienstadt (she vividly lives on in family history as Tante Mimi), at considerable personal and financial cost to the stressed, poverty-stricken refugee family of 1940–1941. Other family members perished as well on the Kuttner-Schocken side; in particular, my paternal grandmother's sister and brother. This was hidden from us.

Safe in America, culturally our family household epitomized the *Bildungsbürgerlische* German Jewish family described so well by historians George Mosse and Paul Mendes-Flohr, among others,[28] and recalled fondly with pride by various Kuttner children and grandchildren. Books everywhere, literary classics leavened with detective stories (my mother's favorites!) and children's books, classical music—the recorded soundtrack of our lives, the grand piano in its place of honor in the living room (our one piece of serious furniture)—music lessons for each of the nine children, higher education a foregone conclusion. To me the internal family structure could be said to harken back as well to an earlier, Eastern European type—the many children, the husband as dedicated Talmudic scholar, days consumed in the intense all-male world of canonists, religious and lay, in his house of studies, nights ensconced in his home study bent over obscure, ancient texts, oblivious to the hubbub around him. And then the

---

28 As George Mosse describes it, "what once had been a part of German culture [a preoccupation with education, self-refinement and high culture, humanism and the Enlightenment] became a central Jewish heritage ... a redefinition of the Jewish substance." Mosse, 77. Paul Mendes-Flohr, for his part, emphasizes the ethical, urban, and cosmopolitan nature of the ideal of *Bildung*, which, he says, "Jews embraced with a single-minded devotion." Mendes-Flohr, *German Jews*, 5. Both scholars, among others, emphasize the paradigmatic German Jewish obsession with Goethe, inspiring me to choose Goethe as the two-edged introductory epigram to this chapter. And as both scholars point out, for German Jews the centrality of *Bildung* and its commitment to enlightened, broadly humanist values persisted long after its subversion and abandonment by a majority culture swept up in the rising tide of extreme nationalism. Mendes-Flohr, *German Jews*, 8–13, Mosse, 73–75.

energetic, forceful wife, ensuring that her husband remain undisturbed while she ran her immense household with verve and aplomb, brilliantly managing the finances. Religiously, we ran Catholic, church every Sunday, Catholic school, withal our maternal German Jewish grandparents, entirely secular, a constant, beloved presence. This is the family home that I knew, with all its inherent contradictions and ambiguities, in the America of the late forties and early fifties.[29]

And yet, there was a darkness about my father, even as he scaled ever more prestigious international academic heights. As many around him knew or surmised, my father suffered from chronic severe depression throughout his adult life in an era that afforded little to no relief through effective medication. Of course there could be many reasons for his periodic depressions: a biological imperative perhaps; the truly traumatic circumstances of his father's death in his childhood; the shock of seeing his intimate and wider cultural world shattered and destroyed; the belated discovery, newly publicized in the aftermath of the war, of the horror of the concentration camps in images all too familiar to us now. I would offer, for purposes of this essay, an additional interpretation.

Diane Jonte-Pace, in her brilliant article entitled "When Throne and Altar Are in Danger: Freud, Mourning, and Religion in Modernity"[30] suggests a reading of Freud, focusing on his 1917 short piece *Mourning and Melancholia*, a reading that casts all of Freud's writings on religion[31] as one long elegy for the lost world that preceded modernity.[32] In *Mourning and Melancholia,* Freud discusses the similarities and differences between the process of grieving or mourning and its more pathological variant, then known as melancholia. Both, he argues, are "a reaction to the loss of a beloved person *or an abstraction* [my italics] taking the place of the person, such as fatherland, freedom, an ideal, and so on. In some people, whom we for this reason suspect of a pathological disposition, melancholia appears in place of mourning."[33] Jonte-Pace goes on to comment: "His [Freud's] definition was broad: it included cultural losses, losses of ideals

---

29 See Appendix III for family snapshots of that era. To me, they read visually as "non- American," "refugees," "foreigners."

30 Diane Jonte-Pace, "When Throne and Altar Are in Danger: Freud, Mourning, and Religion in Modernity," in *Disciplining Freud on Religion*, eds., Gregory Kaplan and William B. Parsons (New York: Lexington Books, Rowman & Littlefield, 2010), 59 – 83.

31 Most notably: *The Future of an Illusion*; *Civilization and its Discontents*; *Totem and Taboo*; and *Moses and Monotheism.*

32 Jonte-Pace, 61.

33 *The Penguin Freud Reader*, ed. Adam Phillips [trans. unspecified] (London: 2006), 310.

like freedom and equality, losses of landed identities associated with emigration, and religious losses."[34]

It is in this way that I like to think about my father, a man unable to mourn, drowning in melancholia for all that was gone, above all for a coherent, multi-cultural, cosmopolitan European civilization forever lost in the horror of war and that he so brilliantly epitomized. Fluent in multiple languages, an accomplished musician, pianist, and composer, a sometime poet, who as a young man gave up what he saw as an ultimately unsuccessful career in music to study law,[35] whole-heartedly embracing a tradition of scholarship to which he so brilliantly continued to contribute, my father resembled, was identical even, to so many other noted German Jewish refugees. In his radical lifelong commitment to the further-ance of a European-based culture in both his professional trajectory and in his personal life, then, I see the German Jew par excellence as cultural stereotype, one among his many peers who survived, extruded from their homeland and their culture in the most violent fashion, yet valiantly struggling to create, to study, to write.

What I also want to propose in my exploration of my private father, the deeply hidden Jew, perhaps even from himself, is the ironically quintessential purveyor, in his accomplishments and in his obsessions, of a very special *Jewish* intellectual tradition. It is significant, I would argue, that he discovered and em-braced his newly adopted religion in a lifelong *scholarly* project, his Catholicism acted out in an almost obsessive involvement with the law, now canon law, as an object of deep study, veneration, and exegesis in what may be seen as a uniquely re-imagined halachic enterprise. His research focused on ancient legal texts and their sources; his work revolved around the arduous attempt to locate, collate, and interpret them both contextually and in the light of a deep, vital tradition. In particular I refer to his essay "Harmony from Dissonance: An Interpretation of Medieval Canon Law."[36] First delivered as a lecture in 1956 and revisited in 1979, this piece, remaining justly famous among canonists,[37] represents his over-arching view of the discipline to which he devoted a lifetime of strenuous effort. The title stems from and pays tribute to the title of Gratian's eleventh-century

---

34 Jonte-Pace, 64, using a slightly different translation of the passage.
35 Stephan Kuttner Interview, 1–21.
36 Stephan Kuttner, "Harmony from Dissonance: An Interpretation of Medieval Canon Law," in *The History of Ideas and Doctrines of Canon Law in the Middle Ages* (London: Variorum Reprints, 1980), 1–16.
37 According to informal anecdotal evidence.

monumental work, *Concordia discordantium canonum.*[38] The correspondence is carefully spelled out: "hermeneutics—the art of reconciliation of sacred authorities—and divine harmony are closely correlated ... . Indeed, in the field of canon law, symphonic rather than architectural structure presents itself much more readily as an adequate symbol."[39] How deeply personal this observation strikes one from the pen of a man who once, after years of serious study, chose music as his first career.

He continues: "In probing the immense detail of regulations, the medieval canonists found, beyond the antinomies of the sources and the antinomies of ecclesiastical institutions, a problem of much deeper concern: the paradox, if we may call it that, of a supernatural mystery which manifests itself in the structural forms of social life."[40] And later, "The mutual penetration of two modes of thought, of supernatural ends and legal means, appears wherever we open the books of the medieval canonists ... . The harmonization of opposites here reaches its supreme purpose, that of integrating human jurisprudence in the divine order of salvation."[41]

Might not these interpretive constructions of medieval canon law overlap with the Rabbinic enterprise, embodied in the Talmud and the Mishnah, its subsequent body of interpretation in the Responsa, reaching back into the *ur*-Deuteronomic text itself? It is in particular in this overlapping, indeed in the identity of the legal, social, and the supernatural realms, in the "harmony" that is the central thrust of this seminal essay and its subject matter, that I see the resonance of an ancient, rich Jewish tradition at the very heart of my father's conversion, transformed into lifelong endeavor. Faith as law, law as faith, a construct that he lived out and embodied, that is what is so Jewish about my father to me.

Finally, of course, and as a link to both the preceding chapter and those that follow, I would submit that in the complexity of his multiple trajectories both personal and professional, I see in my father an embodiment of the complex strands of the Jew in modernity, one that prefigures even, one might say, the postmodern Jew. As many readers doubtless already know, the very phrase "German Jew" or, more abstractly, *"Deutschtum und Judentum,"* was memorably coined in 1915 by Hermann Cohen, the German Jewish philosopher who em-

---

38 In the eleventh century, the monk Gratian, known as the Father of Canon Law, gathered, systematized and applied principles of jurisprudence to the hitherto scattered mass of local canons and papal decrees. See Stephan Kuttner, "Harmony," 4–5.

39 Ibid.

40 Ibid., 12.

41 Ibid., 13.

braced the binary to argue for a constructive interchange between two cultures as a pathway to the formation of a thoroughly modern, deeply humanist state.[42] Beyond the binary, however, as Mendes-Flohr puts it in his penetrating study, going well beyond his rather misleadingly entitled *German Jews: A Dual Identity,* "their identity and cultural loyalties were fractured, and they were consequently obliged to confront the challenge of living with *plural* [my italics] identities and cultural affiliations."[43] Indeed, he goes on, footnoting a 1995 article on postmodern European identity, "German Jewry's articulate struggle to live with a plurality of identities and cultures —which is increasingly recognized to be a salient feature of Western modernity—is a mirror of a larger phenomenon beyond the specifics of Jewish existence."[44] Michael P. Steinberg, for his part, in his 2007 study of modernity and Jewish self-consciousness, highlights the "accuracy and reality in a pattern of contiguous Judaisms."[45] European Jewish modernity, he goes on to argue, in particular, "chose a multicultural option;" an option that facilitated a survival of the culture through the multiple forced dislocations of the twentieth century.[46] Going back further, Steinberg cites Shaye Cohen's book, *The Beginnings of Jewishness,* centered on late antiquity: "Cohen consistently reminds that Jewishness is a 'variable not a constant.'"[47] Notably, Cohen also asserted, "The uncertainty of Jewishness in antiquity curiously prefigures the uncertainty of Jewishness in modern times."[48]

For an even more recent take, I turn to Cynthia Baker's brilliant analysis of the multiple usages of the word *Jew.* In her slim, densely packed volume, Baker pointedly italicizes the term throughout in order "to invite the reader always to read the term with the complex depth and dimensionality it harbors."[49] Historically, she insists, "The question of what *Jew* signifies ... is embedded in very particular ways in the construction and negotiation of foundational categories and

---

42 See by way of discussion, David N. Meyers, *Resisting History* (Princeton: Princeton University Press, 2003), 53–54.
43 Mendes-Flohr, *Dual Identity,* 3.
44 Ibid., 3–4.
45 Steinberg, 1.
46 Ibid., 5. It is interesting, given my father's personal history and overarching theory about his chosen discipline, as shown in his essay on dissonance and harmony cited above, that Steinberg privileges musicality as the dominant metaphor in his re-engagement with the question of Jews in modernity. See. e.g. ibid., 8–11.
47 Ibid., 6. See Shaye J. D. Cohen, *The Beginnings of Jewishness: Boundaries, Varieties, Uncertainties* (Berkeley, California: University of California Press, 1999), 10.
48 Cohen, 8.
49 Baker, xiii.

concerns of Western identities and cultures."[50] Baker goes on to take us, in the concluding portion of her work, into the explosive world of the ever-expanding postmodern *Jew* in all its mutability and multiplicity. "Bids for and claims of ownership; the exercise of naming, defining, and delimiting; assertions, attributions, or disavowals of belonging; and explorations or accusations (including self-accusations) of usurpation, misappropriations, and masquerade—all of these represent the current state of the questions of *Jew(s)* ... in the late twentieth and early twenty-first centuries."[51]

And what has all of this to do with my scholarly father? For one, it solidly situates him well within an ongoing conversation, sometimes or even often fractious, dating from earliest times, on what it means to be a Jew. It is within this conversation that I seek to situate this chapter and indeed my entire monograph. To be sure, Baker refuses to directly engage in the question of exactly "Who is a Jew?"[52] nor do I make any such exclusive claim on my father. I have no wish to downplay his guarded references to his own deeply held religious faith or his patently obvious commitment to the Roman Catholic world that he embraced so ardently. I also must acknowledge that Endelman finds even among "sincere converts" (the term is his)[53] evidence of long-held, now outmoded anti-Judaic and antisemitic supercessionist and universalist tropes.[54] Sadly, this was most probably true for my father as well, a man admittedly formed by patristic theology in his new life.[55] Nonetheless, to me, my father Stephan Kuttner unmistakably forms part of a historical German Jewry, whether or not in good standing, depending on viewpoint, with all the inherent contradictions and ambiguities that the term embraces. Indeed, the profound and complex deracination my father embodied as a German Jew, as I see it, is a way that I, a committed Jew reclaiming her past, have come to understand my father, to forgive him, and to honor him.

---

50 Baker, 7.

51 Ibid., 93; for a more complete discussion, see chapter entitled "New Jews: A View From the New World," ibid., 126–132.

52 See Ibid., 3.

53 See Endelman, *Leaving*, 255.

54 Ibid., 11. In recent times, the Roman Catholic Church in the 1965 papal encyclical *Nostra Aetate* signaled a shift from a hard supersessionism (the belief that the Christian covenant supersedes and replaces the Mosaic one) to a softer note. Nonetheless, supersessionist tropes persist in its liturgy and elsewhere.

55 Stephan Kuttner Interview, 169.

Coda

When I introduced my new beau, Barry Silverblatt, a Jew, to my father in the Spring of 1996, he was already in decline, confined in his last months to a hospital bed in the living room of my parents' condominium and final home. He seemed at peace there, in their strikingly lovely space, the breathtaking sweep of the entire Bay Area before him, the university campanile with its hourly chimes, so European, reassuringly close by. Almost as soon as Barry and I arrived, my father gestured to my mother to bring him a document that turned out to be photocopy of a page from the official register of doctoral recipients (*Album für die Doctoren der Rechte*) for the 1929 – 30 academic year at the University of Berlin. Proudly, he pointed out to my future husband his own name, emphatically defaced, along with several others, self-identified as either Protestant or non-religious (a status he then claimed), with a strongly scrawled *"JUDE."* Somehow with this gesture, I would maintain, at the end of his life my father was able to reclaim his past, his Europeanness, his Jewishness, as a way of expressing his solidarity with the Jewish man he greeted so warmly and who would one day become his future son-in-law, though only, sadly, after his death. Somehow, I am convinced, my Dad was eager to tell Barry that he too was a Member of the Tribe.

Epilogue

In my post-career years, beginning in the fall of 2010, I became deeply involved in the study of Jewish history and culture in a master's program at the Graduate Theological Union's Richard S. Dinner Center for Jewish Studies in Berkeley, California. How happy I was there! After my many all-consuming years of major litigation as a Deputy Attorney General for the State of California, my broader intellectual interests were given free rein as I set forth to explore my family's past in its largest sense, the rich and complex German Jewish world from which my ancestors sprang and in which they all too briefly had thrived.

Vivid memories—I am on my way once again to the University of California library, past crowded student cafes and up through majestic old growth groves and grassy sunlit expanses, dark and light, pierced by joy. These are my father's old stomping grounds, I would say to myself. We are one now, I would say to him silently, with pride, with humility, with gratitude. Finally, I got to reclaim my distant father. I got to see myself as his heir, certainly not in terms of accomplishment, but in terms of his preoccupation with the past, with history, with tradition, and how these wholly inform human life and human society and infuse it with value. I am a Jew, Dad, I say. I am a seeker. I am like you.

Part II

Resonances

In their very different and powerful ways, my parents' narratives spoke strongly to me of the perhaps unanticipated, even unwitting primacy of a Jewish identity, revealed most openly in my mother's oft-repeated, even ritualistic family origin stories, as well as more subtly in my father's profound hermeneutic investment in the relationship between law, society, and the divine. Both of their narratives, I have argued, remain deeply reflective of dominant biblical tropes, echoing persistent underlying cultural patterns, despite the radical break represented by conversion.

I chose the word "Resonances" with care as the title of this second part of my book to honor the orality of what follows, as well as the deep, metaphorical sense of "echo" I have found in these after-narratives. The Merriam-Webster dictionary defines resonance as "the quality of a sound that stays loud, clear, and deep for a long time." It is this quality I sought to explore when, as I had planned all along, I traipsed around the United States and Canada on a long-cherished project to interview my many siblings and our offspring about their relationship to their Jewish ancestry. To be clear, this was a topic we had never discussed among ourselves before. Remarkably, each and every one immediately declared a willingness to cooperate with the project; more than that, almost everyone told me how delighted they were that I was launching it! Already I was encountering a response that raised as many questions as the deceptively simple one ("would you agree to ...") it answered.

I now have twenty-five videotaped interviews that I conducted over an approximately eighteen-month period beginning in April 2014. In their narratives, as set forth in the transcribed excerpts featured in the two following chapters and in Appendix II (somewhat edited and condensed for clarity), the second and third-generation descendants of my converted Jewish parents, almost all raised non-Jewishly, all but one untethered from a formal Catholicism long since abandoned, discuss their relationship to their Jewish ancestry and to a Jewish identity. Their stories revealed the deep impact of my mother's Jewish escape story, the effect of my father's deep moral commitments, and, more often than not, a deeply-felt cultural affinity to the world of the emancipated German Jew as well as, more subtly, to underlying Ashkenazic social and cultural patterns.

Jeffrey Shandler, in a public lecture on his monograph on Holocaust memory, emphasized the role of the interview process on survivors' memories.[1]

---

1 "Tales Retold: Holocaust Survivors on *Schlindler's Lists*," presentation sponsored by the University of California at Berkeley's Center for Jewish Studies on April 10, 2018. See Jeffrey Shan-

https://doi.org/10.1515/9783110731965-008

Katya Reszke, for her part, in her work on identity narratives of third-generation post-Holocaust Jews in Poland, has come to see "the construction of identity as a phenomenology of a narrative nature."[2] Both of these tendencies, I argue, come into play in the diverse voices featured below. Classic archives in the Derridean sense, the oral narratives I present here coalesce into an overwhelmingly *Jewish* story about Jews, my family of Jews. At times uncertain, at times rebellious, yet somehow unmistakably Jewish in whole or in part, our voices embody not only classic Jewish themes of trauma, dislocation, and rebirth but also the oft-unwitting persistence of underlying social and cultural patterns. We can also find in them the uncertainties of identities in transition, arising not only out of the inherent hybridity of a mediated Christian-Jewish milieu, but also out of the exigencies of the interview experience itself. Might we see, then, in the eagerness and even enthusiasm with which so many of my interviewees embraced my project, a desire to uncover and recover an obscured past, to claim it and to own it, to be fully, proudly oneself at last?

---

dler, *Holocaust Memory in the Digital Age: Survivors' Stories and the New Media Practices* (Stanford: Stanford University Press, 2017).

2 Katya Reszke, *Return of the Jew* (Boston: Academic Studies Press, 2013), 51.

3 Sibling Stories

I engage here in chronological order with each of the voices of my seven living brothers and sisters, the second generation, the ones who, like myself, experienced most directly and intimately the full impact of our converted German Jewish parents' presentation of self. For almost all of us, these interviews marked the first time that we talked openly amongst ourselves about being Jewish, about how we saw ourselves as Jewish (or not), and how we got that way. The experience was uniformly experienced as profound. Each of us reflected deeply on our own evolving identities as we had groped our way through our quintessentially liminal family landscape, to emerge, often enough though not always, at the margins of Jewish identity, and yet most often claiming a proud Jewish inheritance and a proud Jewish self. Viewed through overlapping lenses of memory, cultural inheritance, and gender, our narratives weave a complex pattern of transmission.

Ludwig:

I begin with my eldest brother Ludwig, proud ex-Marine, the only surviving full-bore Catholic among us all, and defiantly so at that. Thus, to my routine opening inquiry ("tell us who you are'"), his response: "I was baptized Ludwig George Victor Gerhard Kuttner." Point made!

Ludy, as he is known in the family, first learned of his Jewish heritage as a young child living in Rome. While he spoke the Italian of his surrounding environment, his language at home was German and he knew that his parents considered themselves to be German. When he asked them why they were living in Italy,

> They tied that up with Hitler ... we're in Rome because Hitler didn't like and was persecuting anyone whose ancestors were Jews …. I wasn't particularly bothered by it. I mean, I was a happy little boy.

This willed insouciance persists in his matter-of-fact (and perhaps not always believable) narrative of an carefree trajectory to America at almost six years of age and a rapid, seamless acculturation process thereafter, his Italian rapidly replaced with English. Ludy always thought of himself as Catholic, he says, but pointedly insists he would fight boys who made antisemitic remarks.

https://doi.org/10.1515/9783110731965-009

> Paul Schilke ... would say something about Jews and I'd punch him .... He did it once, because [though I was] a little guy I was a lot tougher than I am now. So, I mean, I enjoyed fighting.

Later on, he recalls

> one antisemitic episode with a boy named Bobby Gouvreau. The Gouvreaus lived across the street from us .... It was right at the time of the establishment of Israel. And I couldn't take on Bobby Gouvreau by myself, because he was three years older. But Andy [Ludy's younger brother] and I took him on. We beat the crap out of him.

He clarifies,

> I didn't identify in the sense of saying I'm a Jew. I identified in the sense—these are people that I come from. It's not about me. It's about my people. They're my people. They're the people I descended from. And I don't like it. I mean, I don't like to hear those kind of remarks.

Calling himself "a fairly orthodox practicing Catholic," Ludy seized upon many moments in his interview to emphasize his strong adherence to his faith. He recalled with enthusiasm his Catholic education (elementary school: "a happy experience:" his Jesuit High School: "intellectually rigorous") and passionately expounded on his adult vision of Catholicism as "a satisfying, structured way to deal with the unknowable." In part perhaps because of his strong adherence to a faith tradition, he sees Judaism primarily as a religion defined by affiliation and practice, and one he does not relate to except as a sort of origin religion, "the precursor of Christianity." During the interview he seemed to reject the concept of a secular Jewish identity and overtly dismissed the notion of a Jewish ethnicity. Our maternal Jewish grandparents (our Oma and Opa) who lived with us, and later down the block, were German, he insists, sharing our typically German Christmas, tree and all. Our relatives in Israel are "Israeli—that's their primary identity in my mind," although, when pressed, "I'm not denying they're Jewish." To Ludy, his Jewish ancestry is very distant—at least three generations back, he insists.

And yet, somewhat inconsistently, a treasured memory and the sole one he brought up of our beloved Oma was what he recalled as her active participation in a postwar organization attempting to reunite Holocaust survivors with relatives.

> Oma in particular had a strong identification with Jews, and worked so hard to put people together. And I [was] so proud of her. It was so beautiful.

Equally surprising to me was a pre-interview email he sent to our entire far-flung family describing our great-grandmother's deportation and death at Theresienstadt (which of course we all knew about). When I asked Ludy why he sent that email, he stated that he wanted people to know that she had died in a concentration camp. He claims a small child's memory of this great-grandmother from family visits, perhaps colored by photographs, he acknowledges. "She was very nice to me and she wore a long, black dress. And we sat in her garden." Interestingly, having aggressively reared his six children as Catholic, he seemed quite accepting of a Jewish turn among several of his children and grandchildren, as set forth in the chapter below.

To me, Ludy's passionate adherence to his Catholic faith mirrors his other great passion, not discussed in the interview—his strong identification with his youthful Marine Corps experience. To this day, he actively participates in Marine Corps events as a (former) uniformed officer and has been known on occasion to sign his communications to us, and most likely to others, with "*Semper Fi*" the Marine Corps motto. I see his two passions as linked commitments to strong, single-minded, all-encompassing institutional hierarchies in all their distinctively American manifestation. Together they seem to have provided a coherent, stable narrative and identity to the young multi-lingual, multinational, unwillingly cosmopolitan (because Jewish!) immigrant child.

What is most striking to me about this interview, and about my oldest brother in general, is his identification with an ethos of rage as his go-to response to antisemitism. Clearly his strongest response to his Jewish heritage, from which he otherwise wholly distances himself, is to "punch," to "beat the crap out of him," to being "tougher" when confronted with antisemitic remarks. "I don't like that stuff, and I don't take it. I never have and I never will." In this, I see Ludy as unconsciously reprising the role of the "muscle Jew," that early Zionist response to centuries of European oppression, overlaid with a general Zionist valorization of militarism as a critical existential choice and a way of situating oneself in the world.[1] (Indeed, now in his eighties, Ludy remains devoted to physical fitness.) He seems to have no knowledge or awareness of the Eastern European *Yeshiva bucher*, hermeneutically obsessed, traces of whom, I have sug-

---

1 Muscular Judaism (*Muskeljudentum*), a term invented by Max Nordau in a speech at the Second Zionist Congress (1898), referred to the ideal mental and physical properties of the new Jew, the Zionist Jew, in contrast to his vision of the traditional Eastern European Jew as physically weak, easily victimized, and obsessed with religious minutiae. See generally, Todd Samuel Presner, *Muscular Judaism: The Jewish Body and the Politics of Regeneration* (New York: Routledge, 2007). Presner locates the origins of the Zionist preoccupation with the "muscle Jew" in a modernist German cultural, social, and political framework.

gested, persist in my father's persona and life choices. Nor is he particularly interested in the Ashkenazi evolution in modernity, originating with Moses Mendelssohn, morphing into the *Gebildete*, the passionately engaged German Jewish intellectual, a type clearly embraced by my father and indeed key to me to his entire outlook and personality. Instead, Ludy's explicit and emphatic claim of inheritance as his father's eldest son is based exclusively on their shared Catholic religious faith.

Susanne:

Next is my older sister Susanne, born in Italy, the baby in my mother's escape story. (My parents' second child, Andrew, died in 1969.) Susanne begins by telling me that she is very enthusiastic about my project and deliberately seats herself in our videotaped interview in front of an impressive portrait of my mother, aged sixteen or seventeen. Susanne was always aware that her parents had to flee Europe because they were Jewish, she says, but to her they were Catholic, ("they went to Church") and German.

> When I think of my identity as a child, it wasn't that my parents and grandparents were Jewish, but [that] my parents and grandparents were foreigners. They were immigrants. They had accents. They spoke a different language; they spoke German.

Regarding her maternal grandparents, she says:

> I knew that they were Jewish, but I only thought of them as German, very German. We saw photographs of Opa with the helmet in the First World War and in his tails and elegant court wear at the settlement at Versailles after the First World War.

In short, it seemed that she had absorbed an earlier, thoroughly assimilated German Jewish sense of self.

Like the rest of us, she grew up isolated from other Jews. She thought of our parents' refugee friends as German as well. As a child, she attributed the uneasy sense of Otherness she felt at her Catholic school to her family's immigrant status. And yet, dark shadows lingered. Susanne worried because her grandparents were not baptized and could not go to heaven. She believed that the Jewish people betrayed Jesus, as she had been taught in school. It was only later, in early adolescence, that she became aware of "looking different," her Jewish body a source of estrangement in the midst of the predominantly Irish Catholic milieu in which we were educated.[2]

Susanne's understanding of who she was began to shift in her teenage years. She began to think of her great-grandmother Dora Ullman's death in a concentration camp, and learned, later on, of the murder of other family members during the Nazi era, and later still, of historical Jewish oppression. All of these things

> made me feel much more connected to being Jewish. Now I say often I come from a Jewish family. Although I'm not a practicing Jew, I'm not a religious Jew, I am very close—I am related to the Jewish experience. Civil rights, racism, all those things I think that I came at passionately partly because of being Jewish.

When Susanne met John, her future husband, a non-Jew, she told him that her family had to leave Germany because they were Jewish. Although she and John baptized their three children and for a time attended services on Christmas and Easter, the family for all practical purposes had left the Catholic Church and provided no religious education to their children, who were sent to public and then private non-denominational schools. Eventually their daughter Martha married a Jewish man in an interfaith service in their home, complete with a *Ketubah* in which the couple pledged to give their children a Jewish upbringing. This remains for Susanne an inspirational experience and she speaks of it often.

Susanne talked at length about two key trips she took to Israel with her husband in conjunction with his work. The first, in the late 1960s, brought nothing but excitement and joy:

> I'm really in the holy land now. I'm at the navel of the universe, a holy place for everyone, overwhelming. I felt like all the streams of my life were together.

A second trip to Israel a few years later turned out quite differently. When questioned in a tourist shop about her Jewish credentials, Susanne responded with her usual qualifiers—"Well I'm Jewish but ... I come from a Jewish family but I'm not ..." The shopkeeper responded by erupting in fury, screaming "how can you call yourself—you're not! You're nothing but a whore!" To my shy, sensitive sister, this remains a traumatic horror story, and, tellingly, where she chooses to end her interview—a final explanation point on a fundamental undercurrent of Otherness, a doubled alienation that runs through her interview. Where does she belong?

---

2 That concern is echoed in our sister Barbara's experience below.

For Susanne, as I see it, her hybrid identity remains a bind, an unresolved conundrum, an intricate and difficult problem that surfaces over and over in the stories she tells about her life and her relationship to Judaism. She feels disrespected by those Jews who reject both her and her beloved parents because of their conversion to Catholicism. The hostile, hate-filled experience she had on her second trip to Israel remains particularly troubling to her. While she does not consider herself Catholic, she remains very attached to her family's secular Christmas and Easter festivities and has evidenced no interest in establishing any Jewish communal ties. And yet she publicly and openly manifests a strong and vigorous pride in her family's Jewish past and sees their experience in the Holocaust as seminal to her sense of self. I cannot help but catch in her troubled tale of the hostile Jerusalem shopkeeper an echo of that long-ago Marrano, Uriel da Costa, the tormented deracinated Jew, in flight from the Portuguese Inquisition, landing in the comparative freedom of seventeenth-century Amsterdam, caught between two worlds, the Christian and the Jewish, unable to ground in either.[3]

A final note. Not long before our interview, Susanne, a classical music lover and for many years a dedicated participant in the renowned Boston Cecilia Choir, circulated among our family a brief and moving documentary film clip featuring a Thereisenstadt survivor. In it, the subject, a classical pianist who briefly plays for us, insists that her music was the key, literally and psychologically, to her survival. To me, the clip epitomizes the experience of the German Jew, the high musical culture, the bitter fate, an experience obviously embraced by Susanne herself as a marker of family identity. Did she know that she was outing herself when she felt moved to circulate this piece?

Angela:

Myself, briefly, next in line. Obviously, this very endeavor and the working out of it in these pages bears witness to my strong relationship to my ancestral heritage. However, to expand the narrative a bit, I agreed to be interviewed myself

---

3 See Uriel da Costa, *A Specimen of Human* Life, trans. Peter Bergman (New York: Bergman, 1967). *Specimen* manifests as a searing autobiographical *cri de coeur* written on the eve of da Costa's 1640 suicide in Amsterdam. The power of his double alienation resurfaces in nineteenth-century Germany in yet another uneasy Jewish-Christian space. See Karl Gutzkow, *Uriel Acosta*, trans. Henry Spicer (London: Kegan Paul, Trench: 1885). See also Angela Botelho, "The Marrano in Modernity: The Case of Karl Gutzkow," in *3 Nexus* (Rochester, NY: Camden House Press, 2017), 123–143.

by my brother Thomas (see below) "to fill out the project," as he put it. In my own interview I elaborate on my hesitant, decades-long approach to my current rich Jewish life with its active synagogue involvement and its fully-engaged investment in Jewish Studies. Salient aspects are, perhaps, a childhood vividly marked by the dimly understood but powerful impact of my mother's family origin tales, the painful inchoate conflicts of my Catholic elementary school years, marked by the overt antisemitism of the era ("the Jews killed baby Jesus, I love baby Jesus, Oma and Opa are Jews"), my Catholic high school's refusal to put up with my rebellious, insistent questions ('what do you mean, the virgin birth?'), so Jewish as it turns out, and my 1963 college trek, while on a junior year abroad in Paris, to Israel to stay with my mother's much beloved older sister, Tante Sophie. I also met other Jewish relatives there, *kibbutzniks*, whom I had never heard of, though they certainly had heard of us. Bemused by our family's turn to Catholicism, they didn't take it too seriously. To them, we were still Jews. Their attitude affected me profoundly. Thereafter followed years of an uncertain, highly charged, fearful attraction ("I know I'm Jewish, but what if they won't accept me because of the Catholic stuff?"), finally resolved in midlife in what turned out to be a profound experience of coming home.

Barbara:

My younger sister Barbara, by way of contrast, bluntly rejects all Jewish identity for herself other than the genetic, putting her at the extreme end of the spectrum of my sibling interviews. She says she dimly became aware of her Jewish heritage when our parents began receiving reparations from the German government in the early 1950s. She does not recall having any reaction to what she calls "the Jewish part" because she felt so strongly that "we were Catholics." She does recall eventually learning about relatives dying in the Holocaust, but felt that it was "my parents' history, not so much my history as their history." Her view today firmly remains the same. "My reaction is that it's part of my family's history, but it's not a part of me." She identifies as "ex-Catholic ... not religious at all ... somewhat anti-religious, actually. I have no patience for it." Although she was married in a Catholic Church to placate relatives on both sides, she already had severed her ties to Catholicism and did not have her children baptized.

As an adult, Barbara's main encounter with Judaism, as she relates, is that "People assume that I am Jewish because of my looks." In response, "I explain that I do not identify as being Jewish" and, depending on the situation, sometimes will explain that "my parents were German Jewish converts to Catholicism who were persecuted by Hitler as Jews and had to flee." When asked to comment on our mother's "sort of autobiography," something I did with all those I interviewed, Barbara reiterated several times that she does not feel any personal connection to the Holocaust and does not "identify it as part of me. I'm aware of the heritage and aware of the family history, but it's not my identity." She refused to be videoed.

I read in Barbara's remarks a sort of latent hostility, rage even, at being *forced* to be Jewish, betrayed by her own body as well as by her family history. In other words, I would say that for Barbara, the experience of being "named" or called out as Jewish, per Derrida and Baker, continues to be experienced as a hostile, intrusive, even violent act, coming from without and in her case vigorously resisted. Nonetheless, as a personal favor to me and so as not to interfere with my project, as she put it, she did agree to be interviewed and was willing to remain honest and forthrightly candid throughout. Like Susanne, she maintains a strong involvement with the traditional classical music canon, a marker of *Bildung* in our family as I related earlier.

Thomas:

At the other end of the spectrum and next in line is my brother Tom, a self-described "pietistic kind of child," trudging off to mass by himself almost every day from a very young age. In high school, influenced by Thomas Merton's writings, his burning ambition was to become a Trappist monk. As he approached his senior year, he drove (in the family's sole automobile) to Merton's Trappist monastery in Kentucky to seek admittance, only to be told he first needed to complete college. As it was already late in the college admission cycle, our father, who actively supported Tom's quest, arranged through one of his priest friends to get him into a Catholic college at the University of Toronto.

Majoring in biblical studies in support of his monastic ambitions, Tom soon moved into the broader field of Near Eastern Studies, where he came under the wing of Frank Talmage, a well-known Jewish medieval scholar, and began to explore his Jewish roots. Talmage was well aware of our father's scholarly reputation and viewed his work as essentially Talmudic; in fact, he opined to Tom, our father could have become one of the great twentieth-century Talmudic scholars. Under Talmage's tutelage, Tom began to study Hebrew, rabbinics, and Rashi. He simultaneously became preoccupied with modern Jewish thought, getting "pulled into the whole German Jewish experience" as he puts it. "I started to identify more and more that really I was a Jew and that I might be a Jew or am I a Jew." After college, at the urging of his mentor, he enrolled in a graduate program at the Hebrew University in Jerusalem. A Jewish colleague of his father at Yale, Judah Golden, arranged a scholarship for him. By then, Tom had abandoned all thoughts of a monastic life, fallen in love, and gotten married.

During Tom's year in Israel (1969 – 1970), he grew very close to his mother's sister Tante Sophie, as we always called her, who became a hero to him.[4] Through Sophie, much like myself six years earlier, he was introduced to other relatives in and out of kibbutz life. By the end of that year, Thomas and his non-Jewish wife decided together that she would convert to Judaism and that they would raise their children as Jewish. Upon their return to Canada, Tom obtained an MA in Islamic studies at the University of Toronto (briefly teaching at a reform synagogue where Gunther Plaut was the chief rabbi) and then began a Ph.D. program in Middle Eastern Studies at the University of Chicago. As the academic job market darkened, the children started to arrive, and the Canadian national health system beckoned, Tom decided to decamp with his family to Toronto, enrolled in law school, and acquired a law degree while completing his Ph.D. examinations at the University of Chicago.

And indeed, Tom did educate and raise his three children as Jews. Unfortunately, the Orthodox and only Jewish *shul* in the small university town of Fredericton, New Brunswick, where he had become a professor of law, recognized neither his wife nor his children as Jewish. The family's Judaism, then, remained exclusively home-based, centering on the Jewish holidays, with Tom instructing his children *ad hoc* in Jewish history and culture. In his professional life, Tom pioneered a course in the history of Jewish civil law, well attended, it turned out, by mostly Muslim students. He was also the driving force and main litigator in a 1996 landmark case on antisemitic hate speech. The case was eventually decided in Canada's Supreme Court, argued and won by Tom. The theory he had developed, to incorporate hate speech cases into human rights protocols adjudged in Canadian administrative tribunals, was adopted by the Court, expanding the standard under which hate speech was adjudicated.[5] Thereafter, Tom's antisemitism legal work became more and more central to his professional life.

In his drive and academic ambition, I would say that Tom resembles his father more than his other sons. Uniquely among his many other children, our father took an active role in his education.[6] Indeed, the impetus behind Tom's return to Judaism reads largely academic and intellectual. While he remains

---

4 Sophie emigrated from Germany to Palestine in 1936, where she was active in developing social welfare programs for orphaned and abandoned children, becoming the beloved *Ima* to hundreds.

5 Ross v. New Brunswick School District No. 15 (1996) 1 S.C.R. 825 (Canada).

6 To me, their lifelong closeness and mutual respect are reflected in the extensive recorded interview process in which Tom engaged my normally highly private and reticent father.

very emotional about the Holocaust (he wept as we talked about our great-grand-mother's death in Theresienstadt), unlike the rest of us, his journey to reclaim Judaism was influenced primarily not by our mother but by our father, the scholar, whom he saw as pursuing an opposite but oddly parallel trajectory from intellectual engagement to a new faith. He states that he feels a deep connection to his father as a scholar and as a man of faith.

In short, Tom's life almost since boyhood evinces a profound attachment to Judaism, deepened not only by a lifetime of study but also by what he sees as core Jewish principles. While recognizing its undeniable importance, he strongly rejects the Holocaust as the center of Jewish identity.

> What I guess bothers me is that it can become, if it's the only thing of salience about Judaism, about one's identity as a Jew, then it seems to me that that's a very weak basis on which to construct a moral life.

To Tom, openly influenced by Rosenzweig, Judaism is a faith tradition, based in Sinai and Revelation, and one that must be embraced by each generation anew.

> I realize that partly driving me was, in terms of my children too, is that there is something greater than this life that they have to be loyal to and responsible to and that that goes beyond just the mundane values of the world. And I do believe that Judaism is a way of doing that, and that since we come from a [Jewish family], there's a long tradition of facing that question about how to behave, and how to be in the world, that's of great value and that's worth continuing.

He acknowledges that he has shied away from all forms of Jewish communal activity. "I just know that, generally, any experience I've had with synagogue life, I've disliked." Instead, he is drawn at times to study in *chavruta* (pairs) and at one point "laid on Tefillin" to study Talmud with a Lubavitcher rabbi. During a sabbatical trip to Jerusalem in 1993, he proudly relates, he was "called to the Torah" at the Western Wall alongside his son David in a private bar mitzvah ceremony.

Today Tom remains unaffiliated, continues to study Jewish history, and in semi-retirement for a long time, has taught the course he developed in Jewish civil law at the University of Windsor, Ontario, his course reader a volume developed by a former deputy president of the Supreme Court of Israel.

Michael:

Next is my brother, Michael, a staunch and serious student of Marxism-Leninism, and among his other political activities, an active anti-Zionist. A transparently good person, he is informed without exception by a high sense of social and moral purpose.

Michael was always aware of his Jewish heritage. "I have a sense that Mom always said to us, 'we're Catholic, but we're also Jewish'. ... She made us feel "that there was something to be proud about, being both those things." He recalls "being taunted as a child" in his Catholic elementary school, "being called 'kike' or Jew-boy – there was naming." Michael's reaction was strong, one of "embarrassment," "hurt." "anger," "shame." He is not sure he told anyone about these attacks. Nonetheless, he recalls, his mother made him feel safe, comforted, and proud of where he came from, reminding him that "Jesus was also Jewish." "She was very strong about being proud of our Jewish heritage. She often talked about the Holocaust, and how they had to flee. We started hearing those [stories] from very early on. I can never think of a time when I didn't know about the Holocaust or about their being refugees from Germany because they were Jewish."

Michael followed his brother Tom to the University of Toronto, where, after completing his college education, which included an academic year in Germany, he settled into a life of political activism and serious commitment to the study of Marxism. (His home study features the complete works of Lenin, I noted). Along the way, he states, he absorbed much of central European history, German Jewish intellectual and cultural life, and the phenomenon of assimilation. It was at this point, and specifically in the context of German Jewish assimilation, that he began to understand his parents and their conversion, he explains.

Michael was quite explicit in explaining a decisive shift in his relationship to his Jewish identity as a result of the Israeli-Palestinian conflict. "My relation to the whole notion of Jewish identity has changed as a result of the Israel-Palestine reality." He became a committed anti-Zionist, remaining careful in the interview to draw a clear distinction between antisemitism and anti-Zionism. As he sees it, the ever-present knowledge that close relatives died in the camps—"our great grandmother and a great aunt in particular"— made him feel even more strongly Jewish and gave legitimacy to the anti-Zionist stance he was increasingly drawn to and which he sees as an integral part of his Marxist worldview. "I never denied having Jewish heritage. I was proud to be a part of people that went through such suffering." As he became involved in anti-Zionist groups in Toronto, "even though I wasn't a Jew according to many of my Jewish friends, I can say that because of what happened to my ancestors and this is all being

done in my name therefore, I have a right to say, 'No you do not speak for me.'"
He began to carry 'Not in my Name' signs at demonstrations in front of the Israeli
embassy in Toronto and experienced serious harassment including being spat
upon.

Michael sees himself as part of the Jewish left and specifically as part of the
Jewish anti-Zionist movement. He recites at will the names of prominent Israeli
and American Jewish revisionist historians and social activists who have influenced his thinking (including such controversial figures as Ilan Pappé, Ivan Ha-
levi, Norman Finkelstein, and Bertell Ollman—all tellingly, for Michael, or perhaps for my benefit, from a Holocaust background). In the end, he says, "my
feeling comes from being a Marxist." I cannot help but think of Isaac Deutscher's
famous essay, *The Non-Jewish Jew*, calling out Karl Marx one of the "great revo-
lutionaries of modern thought" in a list that includes Spinoza, Heine, Rosa Lux-
emburg, Trotsky, and Freud.[7]

In direct contrast to his older brother Tom then, Michael's Jewish identity is
communal and wholly non-religious. He self-identifies as atheist, strongly anti-
clerical, and opposed to all forms of organized religion. Nonetheless, I would
argue, his strong commitment to the Palestinian cause, as he himself states, is
rooted in his Jewish identity and is a marker of it. And so, ironically perhaps,
Michael continues to publicly identify as a Jew in conjunction with his involvement with anti-Zionist causes. Is it too great a stretch to see in Michael the leftist
Jew, the intellectual activist, an inheritor, like his self-identified mentors, of an
uncompromising Ashkenazi political bent, rooted in eastern and central European history, born of the Holocaust? Can we not see another persistent underlying
cultural pattern, surfacing here? Indeed, according to Mosse, "the German Jewish tradition reached its climax in a left-wing identity."[8]

---

7 Ivan Deutscher, *The Non-Jewish Jew and Other Essays* (New York: Verso, 2017), 25–41, 26.
"They had in themselves something of the quintessence of Jewish life and of the Jewish intellect.
They were *a priori* exceptional ... As Jews they dwelt on the borderlines of various civilizations,
religions, and national cultures ... They lived on the margins." Ibid., 27.
8 Mosse devotes an entire chapter to leftist German Jews and their attempt, as he sees it, to con-
cretize ("make concrete") the humanist and universalist ideals of the Enlightenment, enshrined
in the concept of *Bildung*, within modern socialism. Mosse, Chapter IV, "A Left Wing Identity,"
55–71, 55–56.

Francis:

The next brother, born in 1951, was aware as a child of his Jewish background but remained indifferent to it, other than, as he laughingly recalls, the bragging rights he took from his family's Holocaust history.

Francis's moment of reckoning with his Jewish heritage was sudden and traumatic. As he tells it, while serving as a juror at a violin competition in the Bavarian Alps in the 1990s (Francis is a luthier – a maker of string instruments –living and working primarily in Cremona, Italy), he went sightseeing in a nearby town. Wandering into a bookstore, he picked up a small monograph, *Die Juden von Bamberg, 1480–1940*, containing many historical photos. As he recounts it,

> The last photo, I looked at it, and that's when I became aware. Because there was a photo of a woman walking down the street with a police officer, an official behind her, with two little kids. Two little boys. And, it just sent a shiver down the spine. Really like "zzzzz," like- made my hair rise up, and I said well, "that's Mom. That's Ludy and that's Andy" [his oldest brothers, born in Rome]. And I just closed the book, and that was kind of when I knew, from here on in, when anyone asked me what they were, they were German Jews. That was the moment, a moment, decisive, where I definitely said, yeah, I'm. ...

Some years later, Francis was a featured artist in a major violin competition in Paris and was asked to compose a biographical sketch for the exhibit brochure. Francis made a point of making sure to be introduced in the brochure as *né de réfugiés juifs allemands qui ont dû fuir l'Allemagne*. He goes on to comment:

> In Paris I'm always reminded of World War II. I mean, it's just essential. I'm always reminded of the war and everything and the history of it, and the history of France and the Jews. I wanted people to know where I came from. From German Jews who would have been, and were, either left or got massacred. There's a reason I put that in French. For them to feel whatever they want to feel.

Several years ago, Francis claimed a German passport as a right, identifying himself as Jewish in his application papers. He does not consider himself German; instead he insistently and proudly proclaims himself to be a German Jew (which he thinks of as an ethnicity – Francis is fiercely secular and non-religious).

In the summer of 2011 Francis sent a long e-mail,[9] the subject line "Terezin," to all of his siblings[10] as our far-flung family prepared to gather in Berkeley, Cal-

---

9 With several accompanying snapshots, among them one that is now the cover of this book.

ifornia for our first reunion after my mother's death.[11] The e-mail recounts his sudden and impulsive journey to Theresienstadt in the midst of an international conference of violin and bow makers held in Prague. The email text, after a brief introduction, unspools as travelogue.

> On Saturday I decided to skip the group's tour of a castle and brewery, and instead hiked across town to a soviet style train station where I purchased a ticket for Nove Kopisti. I was informed by the hotel concierge that this was the closest train station to Terezin (Theresienstadt in German). At the Prague train station I found out that Terezin was actually 5 km from Nove Kopisti, but I figured that I could cab it once I got there. ... After about an hour and 20 minutes (around 1 pm) we arrived at Nove Kopisti, which to my surprise was a wooden bench, no station, just a road in the fields with a few houses in the distance. At first I was concerned as how to proceed from here (nowhere), but walking along a dusty road towards some houses I came upon a slightly wider two lane road, and after another 20 minutes a sign for Terezin, 2 km. Unknowingly skirting the actual town, I finally arrived at a sign emblazoned with a Star of David indicating a road to the "Crematorium Memorial." Emotions running slightly high, I wandered down a roadway between two lines of popular trees. The parking lot to my right was empty. After a couple hundred yards I came upon a large clearing with a huge Star of David in the middle of a graveyard. The Crematorium was closed (it's open for viewing on days other than the Sabbath). Terezin was not a death camp per se, but there were ovens in use as space and wood became scarce. I walked around the grave site a bit, letting my emotions go. There are many willow trees surrounding the clearing so oddly enough I found myself flashing back to Magog.[12] It is the combination of poplars and willow, and a hot summer day. I had the slightly absurd wish to find Dora Ullman's grave marker, of course there are no names on the countless marking stones, just a number. I had a hard time finding a pebble to place on a stone. After strolling along awhile, I finally found a little rock (much in demand!) and placed it on this marker.

There are so many amazing elements in this deceptively simple narrative. The decision to leave the present behind ("I decided to skip the group's tour") with its alternative non-Jewish history (the castle, the brewery). The outset of the journey "through a very pleasant river valley," the arrival at "nowhere." Then the long trek down an uncertain "dusty road," turning this way and that, each step leading further and further into an alternate reality, the reality of the past. Finally, the destination, "a large clearing with a huge Star of David in the middle of a graveyard." The "empty" parking lot and the "closed" Crematorium as markers of "the Sabbath"—we have entered into Jewish time! The exposition is indirect, ambiguous ("not a death camp per se, but there

---

10 Including a sister-in-law as stand-in for our deceased brother.
11 My father, Stephan Kuttner, died in 1996; my mother, Eva Kuttner, in 2007.
12 Magog, a Canadian town near the Vermont-Quebec border, was the site of wonderfully memorable family vacations during the late fifties and early sixties.

were ovens in use as space and wood became scarce"); the reader has to parse the words, forced to provide for herself, almost unwillingly, the full horror that is only implied. Indeed, the narrator himself has to step back (recoil?) into a simpler, happier family past in redeemed time, the Magog of happy memory, but also, ironically, a biblical place name for the end time. Did we know this when we vacationed there? The journey ends with the classic Jewish ritual, placing a pebble, found with difficulty, an oblique reference to the unseen earlier mourners at this holy site, the "this marker;" a defiant gesture in the face of the anonymity of the "countless marking stones."

Here the travel narrative ends. Separated by a space, a coda takes us back into the technological present.

> When I got back to Cremona I went online to the holocaust victims data base
> and entered her name.
> Dora Ullmann (nee Guttman) born December 31, 1861.
> Deported from Berlin to Terezin in transport 1/20 on July 10, 1942.
> Died (murdered) August 2, 1942.
> I kind of wish Oma and Mom knew that she lasted only 22 days there.
>
> Tante Mimi (Jeanne Illch, Opa's sister) was deported to Terezin on transport 1/45 on August 14, 1942. The database shows that she died at Terezin, although no date of death is given. Somehow I had thought she may have been sent on to Auschwitz, so perhaps the worst was avoided.

The e-mail ends here. "See you all next week! Francis." And so he did.

I ask myself, what prompted this journey, what prompted this narrative, what prompted this group e-mail, why in that moment? Aside from my mother, no one in my immediate family growing up ever discussed the Holocaust or Dora Ullmann and her fate, to my recollection. The e-mail was unexpected, startling, compelling, coming across as a clarion call. And when did my irreverent, irreligious brother learn to speak a Jewish language ("the Sabbath") or pick up such a basic Jewish ritual (the stone on the grave)? How do I read this?

I cannot resist help seeing my brother's e-mail as a quintessentially literary piece—the long hot journey down a dusty unknown road, now suffused in sunlight, into a dark past, a classic hero's quest into the void, the narrative voice in search of an elusive Jewish identity, in search of *where we come from*, in search of the authentic self. I see too my brother's own personal, even heroic act of *zakhor*. Now that my mother, the storyteller, is dead, who will tell the story? A different story but really the same story, of death, destruction, survival, urgently recounted to all of us flourishing to a greater or lesser extent in the new land, at our happy family reunion, fifty or more children, grandchildren, great-grandchildren, and beyond. Remember, Francis tells us. Don't forget.[13]

Philip:

The youngest sibling, Philip recalls learning about his Jewish heritage early on through his mother's repeated and embellished stories of escape from the Nazis. She was always very clear, he says, about being Jewish as a source of mortal danger. Her contempt and anger at the Nazis remained visceral, expressed in her oft-told tale to him and to others (including myself) of tearing out the pages of her German passport, infamously marked with a J and the generic name Sarah, to use as all-purpose toilet paper on the ship that took the reunited family from Lisbon to America.[14] Philip remained fascinated by the sharply contrasted narrative rhythms of the narrow escape from danger and sure death to the blissfully safe haven of America, my mother's defiant gestures a common thread. By the time he was ten, he had read William Shirer's *Rise and Fall of the Third Reich* in its entirety.

Philip remained quite close to his mother well into adulthood, and I learned a few new stories about my mother during the course of his interview. For example, she recounted to him with glee her subversive acts as a privileged young

---

13 Some nine years later, in early February 2020 just before the pandemic struck, Francis emailed us all again, this time under the subject line "Elderly Woman at Terezin." The entire email consists of a photograph of a sketch of a bent over and forlorn woman from an exhibit in the airport at Milan. A closer examination of the photograph reveals that it is the watercolor sketch by the Czech-Jewish painter Malva Schalek who died in Auschwitz in 1944. The piece is entitled "Rest. The Thersienstadt Ghetto, 1942–1944." Of course our great-grandmother immediately leaps to mind—it could be her portrait! Francis's intention is obvious. *Zakhor*, Francis reminds us yet again. He has not abandoned his mission.

14 They traveled on the Portuguese ship SS Quanza, leaving Lisbon on August 8, 1940 with 317 passengers, of whom a little more than a third were Jews desperately fleeing Europe. Seventy-eight years later, in April 2018, my great-grand-nephew, Joshua Lefkow, grandson of Ludwig, son of Jessica, posted on Facebook a moving testimonial to the family's Quanza trajectory, including a snapshot of a ship's manifest listing family names. The Quanza had quite a checkered history. Upon reaching New York, 121 passengers, most of whom were Jewish, were denied entry due to their uncertain visa status. The matter became controversial, with major Jewish organizations and eventually Eleanor Roosevelt taking up the refugees' cause. Following an intervention by President Roosevelt, most of the remaining passengers were eventually issued visas. See en.wikipedia.org, SS Quanza, accessed September 26, 2019. Because my family was traveling under a Vatican visa, they were permitted to enter at the ship's original docking in New York. See http://blog.richmond.edu/lawlibrary/?p=1069

Jewish girl, growing up in an increasingly politically hostile Berlin. Often taken for Aryan, with her light hair and blue eyes, she made a point of dancing with a despised, dark-haired Jewish boy at a party rather than with a handsome Nazi youth and enlisted her girlfriends to do the same. Playing off her blond looks, pointedly summoning the Jew within, this was a gesture my mother was to repeat and transpose at her initiation into the Catholic world. Elaborating on her wedding day, she tells Philip, having been required to utter the pro forma "Heil Hitler" at the prior civil wedding registry, she insisted on having Felix Mendelssohn's already-banned wedding march played at her private religious wedding ceremony, subverting the Catholic overlay.

On camera, Philip wept as we began talking about the Holocaust. He spoke at length about the traumatic impact on our mother and especially on Oma of her mother Dora Ullman's fateful death at Theresianstadt, his tears a sort of transferred trauma. Philip emphasizes that his mother never denied her Jewish origins. As an example, he recalls a stint as a young teenager in Rome where his parents were on sabbatical. While they were there, his mother spoke forcefully about the Jewish prohibition against walking under the Arch of Titus, erected in Rome in 70 CE to commemorate Titus's destruction of the Temple in Jerusalem.

> And the way she said it, you know, I don't think she said "we Jews," but it was very clear that that included us, you know, that we should never walk through that arch.

For Philip, the issue of his Jewish identity became more freighted as he moved through adolescence. He attended a purportedly non-denominational, all male prep school from grades seven through twelve in New Haven, Connecticut, where our parents were then living. About thirty percent of the students were Jewish, he estimates. There, he says, the Jewish students thought he was Jewish, the non-Jewish students not so much. As he toggled between two worlds (Philip was then still a nominal Catholic), he remembers difficult antisemitic encounters. In one, a student referred to another student as "a filthy Jew." Philip, upset and angry, took him on. "Well, you know you're talking to one, buddy. My ancestors were Jewish, I come from a Jewish family. You can't talk to me like that!" he recounts. In another incident, when the class award for academic achievement went to a non-Jewish student although his own grades were higher, Philip, intensely competitive, complained to his mother. She took up the matter with the headmaster, who brushed her off, "probably because he's an antisemite," she told Philip. The memory still rankles.

By mid-high school, Philip had become a serious and gifted pianist. At one point during that time, his much-revered elderly piano teacher, seeking to elicit a more nuanced musical interpretation, instructed him, "You need to express a little more, [but] not like those Jewish pianists! [Pause] You can always tell, you know. The nose." Shocked and dismayed, Philip remained silent, swallowing his shame, and continued studying piano with this teacher. Already he had internalized the lesson of hiding, the lesson of shame, the pain of a dual identity.

Philip felt most at home at a music camp in Massachusetts, Merrywood Music School, which he attended as an adolescent for several summers, first as camper and then as counselor. The vast majority of its staff and students were secular non-observant Jews, he reports. Together they shared a passion for music; indeed, Merrywood, he says, was the closest he ever got to a sense of community. People there assumed he was Jewish ("a lot of people think I look Jewish"), and yet he remained at that time sort of a hidden Catholic, though no longer by belief or practice. "I'm more comfortable with ambivalence than with certainty," Philip wryly reflects.

Today, Philip calls himself "half-Jewish," which he defines as Jewish by descent but not by upbringing or belief. He feels comfortable saying "I am Jewish," which he sees as one of the many facets of who he is, but not with "I am a Jew," differentiating between what he calls a social and an essentialist construct.

> Nothing made me feel more like a Jew than to have this [adolescent anti-semitic] experience [with his piano teacher]. So antisemitism for me, when I encounter antisemitism, I feel like a Jew. When I go to a synagogue, I feel like I'm an imposter."

Philip remains distanced from any involvement with Jewish practice or any formal Jewish community. In his persistent embrace of ambivalence, his chosen comfort zone, I cannot help but once again decry, faintly perhaps, ahistorically certainly, the shadow of the alienated Marrano so strikingly described by Yovel.

Reflections

The enormous volume of Holocaust testimony has become a subject of debate among historians as to the relationship between history and memory.[15] Thus, for example, Michael P. Steinberg, in his impressive volume *Judaism Musical and Unmusical*, argues that "the desire to merge history and memory has repressed the substantial tensions that persist between the tropes," proposing instead, "an active dialectic" between the two as a way to achieve "historical un-

---

15 For a wide-ranging discussion, see Susannah Radstone and Bill Schwartz, eds., *Memory: Histories, Theories, Debates* (New York: Fordham University Press, 2010).

derstanding."[16] Eva Hoffman, for her part, pointing out that "the era of [Holocaust] memory is ending,"[17] calls on us, the second or "hinge generation," "to return the *Shoah* . . . to the *longue durée* of previous and subsequent history."[18] My own attempt to contextualize my family's German Jewish history and its aftermath draws on this very impulse. To return to Michael Steinberg, his nuanced discussion expounds at length on the complex interaction between the analytical and the impressionistic, the objective and the subjective, as a way and a process of recovering the past.[19] In Steinberg's formulation, "Memory is staged as raw evidence, to be examined according the rules of historical reasoning."[20] My own investigation of family narratives as coded Jewish identities in the wake of the *Shoah* falls within this rubric. Thus I invoke the voices of my siblings, and in the next chapter, of our children, to examine the persistence of Jewish identity among converted German Jews and their descendants as part of a larger ongoing inquiry on the multiplicities of Judaisms in a post-Holocaust, postmodern era.

In 2008 Marianne Hirsch, a feminist scholar at Columbia University, notably coined the term "postmemory" to describe "the relationship of the second generation to powerful, often traumatic, experiences that preceded their births but that were nevertheless transmitted to them so deeply as to seem to constitute memories in their own right."[21] She clarifies that postmemory' "is not identical to memory [but rather] ... approximates memory in its affective force."[22] Central to her concept, Hirsch highlights "the role of family as a space of transmission and the function of gender as an idiom of remembrance."

Leslie Morris, for her part, in the concluding essay of the volume she co-edited with Jack Zipes, valorizes the terms "postmemory" (borrowed from Hirsch) and "postmemoir" (in fact, they serve as title to her article) as appropriate lenses with which to capture the postwar German Jewish experience. Indeed, Morris utterly rejects the well-worn concept of "German-Jewish symbiosis," notwith-

---

16 Steinberg, 178.
17 Eva Hoffman, *After Such Knowledge: Memory, History, and the Legacy of the Holocaust* (New York: Public Affairs, 2004), 242.
18 Ibid., 198–199.
19 Steinberg, 193–200.
20 Ibid., 194.
21 Marianne Hirsch, "The Generation of Postmemory," *Poetics Today* 29, no. 1 (Spring 2008): 103–128.
22 Ibid, 109. See also, Hirsch, *The Generation of Postmemory: Writing and Visual Culture after the Holocaust* (Columbia University Press, 2012); Hirsch, *Family Frames: Photography, Narrative, and Postmemory* (1997).

standing that the term figures prominently in the title of the volume she co-edited and in which her article appears.[23] Thus, Morris insists on "the impossibility of this term," allowing "neither for the possibility of a (former or present) symbiosis between Germans and Jews, nor the possibility of "pure" or even "real" memoir. Instead, she argues, the Holocaust "seeps into the imaginary of other cultures (and other geographical spaces) as postmemory and postmemoir." Her essay, then, examines "the remnant and the echoes and the ruin of the symbiosis in texts that push at the borders between fact and fiction, documentary and memoir."[24]

And thus we come to my own work and the uncertain fluidity inherent in its form, its subject matter, and the lived experience of its many voices. I use the lens of memory—my own and all our memories of my mother's stories, in themselves memories of her own past—to elaborate on the notion of identity, its fluidity, its persistence in various ultimately creative forms. Unlike Hirsch, then, my primary thrust is on the link between memory, narration, and identity, that is, the central role of storytelling as a form of cultural imprinting and cultural engagement, in itself a seminal Jewish trope, evidenced here in the manifold narrative voices engaged, I would argue, in an act of *Writing the Jewish Self.* Among other things, then, my work has the effect of re-gendering our family history from the public narrative surrounding the celebrated achievements of my scholarly father, Stephan Kuttner, to the private space of the home and our mother's endless, poetic, quasi-obsessive retelling of our family's origin story in Hitler-land, her trajectory from oral to written form recapitulating the birth of our ancient Jewish texts. And in focusing, as I do, on persistent underlying cultural patterns, I seek to capture the remnants, the echoes, in Morris's words, the shards, in another formulation, of the notably complex identity of the German Jew, doubly compromised, as here, by a fleeting Christian overlay.

Culturally, I would also argue that my mother's persistent voice, "tangled up in blue," to quote another Jewish wanderer, recaptures the voice of the Ashkenazi woman as matriarch, ruler of the domestic sphere, carrier of Jewish culture in the home, skillful manager of family finances, counterpoint to the dominant patriarchal mode.[25] (I am reminded of how much my mother controlled the

---

23 Leslie Morris, "Postmemory, Postmemoir," in *Unlikely History: The Changing German-Jewish Symbiosis, 1945–2000*, eds. Leslie Morris and Jack Zipes (New York: Palgrave, 2002), 291–306.
24 Ibid., 291–292.
25 See for an earlier period, *The Life of Glückel of Hameln: A Memoir*, trans. and ed. Beth-Zion Abrahams (Philadelphia: The Jewish Publication Society, 2010). Glückel (1646–1724) was the mother of twelve children and her husband's business and financial advisor and partner. At the age of thirty-seven, following her husband's death, she single-handedly continued to man-

purse strings, handing my father his lunch money as he disappeared each morning from our lives into his house of studies.) I also see my mother as guardian and promoter of *Bildung*, that cultural value so tightly embraced by assimilating and assimilated German Jews. Her household remained filled with classic literary works along with the ever-present sounds of classical music, transforming the realm of male cultural domination (after all, it was men wrote the books and music!) into the stuff of her life with her children.[26] Resonances! Thus the obsession with music, so typical of the assimilated German Jew, ostensibly part of the male realm, including my father's youthful preoccupations, was in fact introduced and reinforced in our daily lives by our mother, to become a professional preoccupation for at least two of her sons (Francis and Philip) and a cultural marker for the rest of us in another instance of gender models reversed. And then, a sweeping intellectual rigor as core to a fully-realized moral life, that legacy of my father, echoing all unconsciously, I have argued, his rabbinic predecessors, become central to two of his younger sons, Thomas, the teacher and scholar, and Michael, the leftist intellectual activist Jew, inheritor of an uncompromisingly secular Ashkenazi political bent, serious student of Marx, claiming Erich Kuttner, my paternal grandfather's cousin and noted Jewish socialist activist, as ancestor despite their leftist ideological differences.[27] Myself perhaps, inheritor of both models as I valorize gender as an idiom of remembrance and family as an engine of transmission in my exploration of a specific historical sub-subculture, the German Jew in conversion, to propose yet another paradigm in the age-old quest to explore and define Jewish identity.

Remarkably then, I find that we, the second-generation descendants of the converted German Jewish couple Stephan and Eva Kuttner, emerge from an ostensibly Christianized context to embody in our own idiosyncratic ways a complex, hybrid but nonetheless unmistakable Jewish identity however tenuously understood, most frequently held outside of any normative practice or affiliation. Jews at the margins, perhaps, and yet insistently, specifically affirming a persistent underlying Jewish culture and identity, an echo of a phenomenon dating

---

age her large family and his far-flung business ventures. For the modern German Jewish context, see Marion Kaplan; see also Paula E. Hyman, *Gender and Assimilation in Modern Jewish History* (Seattle: University of Washington Press, 1995).

26 To this day I cannot hear a Mozart, Shubert, or Mendelssohn recording without my mother's clear, passionate soprano ringing in my ears, her voice echoing the dominant musical motifs as she went about her never-unending domestic tasks.

27 Erich Kuttner was to die at Mauhausen in 1942. A prominent socialist activist and politician before and after the First World War, he continued his strong political engagement in Holland and briefly in Spain after fleeing Germany in 1933.

back some 6,000 years. As Melissa Raphael, Jewish feminist historian and theologian, insists, "Jewishness is not a matter of assent of faith or intellect, but of culture, history, and above all, soul."[28]

Epilogue

I call to mind all the bright interview faces of my brothers and sisters and my heart seizes up. I mean all of their faces, even the ones who doubted the most. They all talked to me freely about their own idiosyncratic form of Jewishness and their closeness to or distance from it. Their voices ring in my ears. After a long, deep silence,[29] we talked about it, we finally talked about it, we finally talked about being Jews! Word is out.

----

28 Melissa Raphael, "Goddess Religion, Postmodern Jewish Feminism, and the Complexity of Alternative Religious Identities," *Nova Religio: The Journal of Alternative and Emergent Religions* 1, no. 2 (1998): 198–215: 201.
29 I am thinking of Helen Fremont, whose family story differs in marked ways from my own, but nevertheless resonates with its Holocaust origins, its (failed) Christian conversion, and its pronounced silences. See Helen Fremont, *After Long Silence: A Memoir* (New York: Delacorte, 1999).

4 The Third Generation: Points of Light

And so, finally, we come to the third generation, those who knew their well-loved German Jewish grandparents at a remove and yet remained indelibly marked by them, not only by their strong personalities but also by the magnitude of their experience as German Jews in flight and as German Jews in double exile.

What I find most striking about the third generation's multiple voices is that by the time I interviewed them, then ranging in age from their late thirties to mid-fifties, their convoluted Jewish heritage had in one form or another assumed a central focus in so many of their lives. In the meantime, the Catholic overlay had all but disappeared, reflecting and amplifying a process that had begun a generation earlier. The shapes of the refracted Jewish identities that emerge remain incredibly diverse, and yet they reflect certain overlapping facets to form a notably *Jewish* constellation, at the edge of the known Jewish universe. Points of light. Barely discernible perhaps from the center, and yet strangely compelling, their images swim into sight in a configuration that can be best understood, perhaps, in the context of a Judaism in postmodernity so beautifully theorized in the work of Cynthia Baker and of Leslie Morris. This Judaism in flux, I would further argue, likewise reprises an ancient lineage of change, of transformation, linked, created even, as always, by the narrative voice, by story.

In the narratives that follow then, selected interviewees unspool their own Jewish stories, bringing life, vitality, and nuance to each embodied experience.[1] Their idiosyncratic voices, linked by a shared conflicted background, reflect not only the multiplicity and fragmentation characteristic of the landscape of the postmodern Jew, they also reinforce for me the dominant theme of my work; that is, the near impossibility of conversion, of being born again, as a project involving Jews. I was struck by Hannah Arendt's comment, in her fine provocative study of Rahel Varnhagen, that Rahel could not be born again.[2] Reaching broadly, I would posit that a Jew cannot be born again because Judaism is not only a religion; indeed, it can be said to be not a religion at all but a social condition, an Othering, as various cultural critics have noted, among them, Aamir Mufti.[3]

---

1 Alas, for reasons of space I have not been able to include each and every one of my eighteen third-generation interviewees in the main body of this text. Basing my decisions on those voices that most fulsomely exemplify the narrative threads I pull out and discuss below, I have placed the remaining excerpts in Appendix II. I strongly urge the reader to consult these texts in order to round out this portrait of a modern Jewish family in flux.

2 Arendt, 253.

3 The Introduction to Cynthia Baker's book offers a fine historical perspective to this concept. For a post-colonial take, focusing on George Eliot's late nineteenth- century novel *Daniel Deron-*

https://doi.org/10.1515/9783110731965-010

Reaching further back in time from Mufti's postcolonial take, we find too in these narratives arising out of a family conversion history hints of the ambivalence and double consciousness of the Marrano, elegantly parsed by Yirmiyahu Yovel. Indeed, an insider-outsider narrative predominates, a balancing act embraced by many yet also for some difficult to sustain. In this deep dive then into the hitherto almost wholly unexplored world of the converted German Jew and its impact on later generations, my work reinforces a nuanced take on Jewishness and specifically on German Jewishness as a culture of internal and external exile, of translation, transformation, and rebirth.

A Radical Alterity

How then to tell the story of the third generation?[4] I begin with the classic, with alterity, alienation, here a compounded radical Otherness. For my Jews here are always, fatally, "Other" Jews, marked by conversion, cast adrift, it would seem, by events over which they had no control, by decisions made two generations ago on a distant continent in a bygone era. Let us consider two of the most striking voices, coming from distinctively different family backgrounds, in order to explore the complicated turns this double distancing can take.

Abigail

We first hear echoes of this radical Othering in the voice of my daughter Abigail. Raising her outside of any Jewish practice or content, still struggling with my own relationship to Judaism, all that I had to give her was to tell her, insistently, repeatedly, that she was Jewish, without more. Her reaction:

> There were so many Jewish people where I grew up [in Berkeley, California]. I knew what their families were like and what they did for holidays, and that was not at all my experience. So I kind of was like, well I don't really understand how we're Jewish.

---

da, see Aamir Mufti, *Enlightenment in the Colony: The Jewish Question and the Crisis of Post-Colonial Culture* (Princeton: Princeton University Press, 2007), 91–110. As Mufti insists, "the consciousness split in two has, of course, been one of the most persistent signs, and recurrent modalities, of elaborations of minority discourse and experience, from Rahel Varnhagen to W. E. B. Dubois and beyond." Ibid., 104.

4 The reader may want to consult the "Family Cast of Characters" at (unmarked) page ix in order to situate the many voices featured here and in Appendix II.

The result for her was an overwhelming sense of confusion, a confusion she acknowledges to this day about her Jewish identity. Indeed, the word "confusing" comes up frequently in her interview. All that she had by way of Jewishness was her grandmother's Nazi escape stories. And to her understanding,

> [They] weren't really Jewish, and didn't celebrate the Jewish holidays. So I felt like what we had as Jewish is just the scary, bad people are going to come get you, and that is Jewish. This sense of well, you're really Jewish, just in case somebody comes to get you, which is kind of not the most pleasant way to think about a part of yourself. There wasn't a lot of what's positive about it, or what would be good about it. Why the heck would you want to identify with that?

And so my naming of her as a Jew turned out to be an incomprehensible blow, an assault that she had no way of processing. Once again we confront the psychic threat, the destructive potential of the Jewish *naming*. We find echoes of Derrida's violence imposed from *without*, the literal one of the Holocaust, but also imposed from *within*, called out by Seidman, an intrafamilial inscription imposed both indirectly through her grandmother's stories and directly by the explicit naming I imposed upon her without (alas!) more. What she did glean was

> There's this mythical girlfriend. This mythical Italian mistress is the reason my entire family exists. That's pretty crazy. Most people don't have that. When I'm talking about all the Jewish people I grew up with, very Jewish because they were culturally Jewish, and they celebrated certain holidays, and they had bar mitzvahs and stuff, but my family was almost killed by the Nazis. So we're kind of Jewish too, but in a very different way. Like totally different. We're so lucky to be here because of this mythical Italian girlfriend. It's weird. It's a weird heritage. It's unusual.

Not surprisingly, the Holocaust lingers. Abby bursts into tears when she read the first iteration of what was to become the first chapter of my book.

> I identify with Grandma as a mother. It was so horrible to imagine that, being a young mother and having to make these—just how scary and horrible things were.

She named her first-born, a girl, after her grandmother.

To Abby the core of being Jewish, always for her identified as "the Jewish religion," is Jewish holiday observance. (In this of course she echoes many American Jews.) To my surprise (and obviously, chagrin), she occasionally has voiced a regret that she wasn't raised "religiously Jewish."

> It would have been easier; a little less confusing. I don't know what to tell my children because I am confused. My husband is the exactly same way. Weirdly enough, I married someone who has the exact same thing: half Jewish, didn't grow up in any religion, no Jewish

culture, but yet at school was called a Jew by the other kids. And that's confusing because he was like "But I'm not really Jewish. I mean, I am, but I'm not."

Today, resolutely non-religious, adamantly opposed to all forms of organized religion, she and her husband refuse to participate in the Jewish holidays, instead embracing an extravagant secular family Christmas in what for them is a shared comfort zone of childhood memories.[5]

And yet. "I have a very Jewish last name now. It's Frank." Abigail appreciates the irony. She laughs. "The most famous Jew in the world right now is Anne Frank and now I'm a Frank." Despite her enormous sense of distance from what she perceives as a more or less unitary Jewish world, linked together by Jewish holidays in which she has no interest and which strike no resonance, she nonetheless seems to find a certain comfort in being considered a Member of the Tribe. "Maybe there's other people who are Jewish out there who are like, 'Oh cool, you're one of us' and that's great if they think that. It feels good." She also feels grounded in the extended Kuttner family and in what she perceives as their own separateness from traditional Jewish life. "The way that I am fits in that family." Nonetheless her strongest identity, and the one she has embraced, is that of the ultimate Outsider, the Other of the Other, the product, perhaps, of a persistent, self-internalized American Jewish cultural gatekeeping.

> I'm much more comfortable with being kind of outside a lot of this. I'm happy to have married someone who is also outside of all of those things so we can be outsiders together. And more and more there's more people that way.

We could situate Abby, then, in her radical refusal of categorical identifications, in her embrace of multiplicity, in her insistence on the non-binary, within the contours of Baker's extended profile of the postmodern Jew:

> a performance of Jew that is not only is a version of a postmodern 'fractured' self or self-divided subject, but also instantiates a multiple or plural sense of self: one that is, perhaps paradoxically, both unsituated and multiply positioned.[6]

I am reminded too, as in many of the interviews that follow, of the thoroughly gendered transmission of trauma featured in Marianne Hirsch's postmemory work, here extended out into the third generation. What remains most striking

---

5 My parents, like so many German Jews, staged an annual elaborate Christmas tree celebration each year, complete with apples, cookies, and lit candles strung on a gigantic *Tannenbaum* in their huge, beamed living room.

6 Baker, 93; see also, ibid., 126–132.

to me, however, is the centrality of the Outsider in Abigail's narrative, or, more precisely, in a term I invent here, the experience of being "the Other of the Other," a doubling of alienation. It is a theme that resonates with the other family narratives above and below. Compared to theirs, Abigail's sense of isolation is more pronounced, more anguished perhaps, more angry it seems, but equally deriving for me from persistent cultural tensions within the Jewish world between a highly secularized German Jewish past in which converts withal remained an integral part of a Jewish landscape (one only has to think of Rosenzweig's family)[7] and the quite different Eastern European landscape that undergirds the experience of most American Jews.

The ironies abound. As I write today amidst the chaos and uncertainties of the 2020 presidential election season, Abby is in the midst of applying for a German passport for herself and her children, a right accorded to her under German law based on her grandparents' 1941 deprivation of German citizenship *qua* Jews. In the end, then, her embrace of family as grounding, along with her own all too real historical grounding, leads both Abby and us back to that larger community of German Jews, transhistorical, transnational, neither here nor there, in translation, as it were, as she herself is.

David

Coming from a completely different background, her cousin David's Jewish tale is equally convoluted. Son of my brother Tom (who as the reader will recall decided early on to raise his children as Jews), David never felt anything other than Jewish. Nonetheless, his Jewish story is complex. Growing up in Fredericton, New Brunswick, in a town where the local (and only) *schul*, an orthodox one, refused to recognize the family as Jewish, his was an essentially piecemeal Jewish upbringing. The family celebrated the Jewish holidays, his father providing instruction in Jewish ritual and history. David learned "Old Testament" stories from Hendrick Van Loon's storybook version,[8] read to him by his father, in what seems to me paradigmatic of his family's persistently attenuated connection to mainstream Judaism (Van Loon was a Christian). David gradually learned

---

7 It is worth noting that most (but not all) contemporary historians of German Jews do not draw a bright line between converted and other Jews.
8 It is worth taking a look at Van Loon's self-illustrated volume, *The Story of the Bible* (New York: Boni & Liveright, 1923) to get the flavor of David's instruction. Van Loon's book, written it seems for children and young adults, reflects the Christian canon, including of course the New Testament.

of his family's Jewish history and acquired a well-developed fear of the Nazis at a young age.

This quasi-radical isolation changed when an almost thirteen-year-old David went to live in Jerusalem with his parents in what turned out, unsurprisingly, to be a crucially formative experience.[9] He made his bar mitzvah at the Western Wall, the event orchestrated by his Israeli second cousin, Tante Sophie's daughter Hannah. David appreciated the event for its simplicity and lack of ostentation, comparing it unfavorably to similar Jewish rites of passage in North America. An Orthodox rabbi, originally from Winnipeg, Ontario, was summoned, complete with full beard, *peyot* (sidelocks), a raft of children, and a devotion to ecstatic song and dance, to provide instruction and eventually preside. David grew to admire the authenticity of this man and his tradition, all the while forming an impression of Israel as an essentially secular Jewish society.

The crisis in David's experience of Judaism came to a head during his college years at McGill University in Montreal, where he encountered for the first time a sizable, vibrant Canadian Jewish community of varying denominations, all with strong local ties. Majoring for a time in Jewish Studies, he found almost all of his fellow students were Jewish.

> At that point, I was confronted with the fact that my exposure to the North American Jewish community was extremely attenuated. It wasn't relatable, first of all, because I was not religious at all. They would have had that upbringing which I didn't have. And their whole social circles, their dating circles—they had gone to school together, so all their friends are Jewish. So there was for the first [time] the realization that I was not about that, that I was very foreign to that culture. *I also realized that Jews don't consider me a Jew* [italics added].

The students in his program were friendly, he says, but he is clear that in their endless conversations about identity, he was viewed as an outsider and fundamentally "not Jewish." His best friends continued to be from his hometown in New Brunswick and were either of Middle Eastern or Italian origin.

> These were the people I identified with much more. We had similar experiences in the sense that in Fredericton, we didn't experience meaningful racism in any way, but we're obviously not Anglo-Saxon. The commonality was being not Anglo-Saxon.

He found an intellectual footing during this admittedly shaky time in his studies of the Frankfurt School when he re-oriented his program toward a modern European focus.

---

9 His father Tom was on a half-sabbatical.

> For me, Theodor Adorno was a revelation because he had the statement—you know, he's half-Jewish—and in a different milieu, but also he says— somewhere he wrote "Well I'm a Jew to the Christians, and I'm a Christian to the Jews," meaning the Other to the Jews. So you have this lack. It's a double anomie.

Like Abby and George, David and his wife (a non-Jew) decided not to raise their two children in any religious tradition. David considers his children to be one-quarter Jewish and plans to tell them about his family background when they are older. He considers Judaism to be an ethnicity and surprisingly, regretfully even, one that does not include his mother, despite her ritual conversion. Nonetheless, David continues to self-identify as a Jew, and espouses an allegiance to secular Zionism.

> But it's strange when the other Jews don't consider you a Jew. My wife considers me to be Jewish but my good friend Steve [a Jew] doesn't.

He retains his youthful admiration for Adorno and feels a personal connection to notable secular Jewish pioneers of modernity, specifically mentioning Freud, Marx, and Einstein, all secular German or Austrian Jews, Marx of course from a converted German Jewish family.

The most striking thing, then, about David's relationship with Judaism, and what he articulates so clearly, is the double alienation, the double Othering, "the double anomie" that he painfully, it seems, experienced and continues to experience.

Indeed, what links these two seemingly disparate narratives, Abby's and David's, is that their deepest and most painful experience of their Jewishness is the compounded double Othering in which Jewish gatekeeping, we must note, unconscious or deliberate, plays a decisive role. An Othering called out by critics as diverse as Cynthia Baker and Amir Mufti as the core of the Jewish experience has become for both David and Abby their own core experience as Jews, well beyond religion, ritual, or history. The Other of the Other. Vividly called out so long ago by Rahel Varnhagen, this indelible socially-conditioned marking has irrevocably marked these cousins in what to me is a shared identity despite their almost opposite upbringing in terms of Jewish education.

Jewish Marriages

Noteworthy too in this generation is the number of marriages to Jews of various stripes[10] in what can be seen perhaps as a conscious or unconscious working out of a sense of family, of familiarity, of belonging. Can we see in this phenomenon a sort of underground healing or quest, a way to still the inner conflict, the inner confusion? While it appears that for some the impetus to take a Jewish partner was compelling, for others a specifically Jewish motivation remained more subliminal. And yet each of these unions forced a reckoning with an ancestral Jewish identity that long predated my interview project, a reckoning both profoundly internal ("Am I Jewish?" "How Jewish am I?") and external ("How are we going to raise our kids?" "What will we tell them?").

Stephan K

Thus we have Stephan K, my brother Ludwig's oldest son. Stephan recalls a pivotal dinner table conversation about his family's Jewish ancestry and his grandparents' escape story.

> I think it was in 1966. I was in elementary school in Washington, D.C. and we were discussing World War II. The Holocaust came up. Something I'd never heard about. It stunned me, it shocked me. At the dinner table I was shocked to find out that—my father said "Oh, yes, some of those people who were killed were even your family." I remember feeling that *in some ways I didn't know who I was all of a sudden* [italics added].

He continues:

> You know, I was born on a Marine Corps base. So my main question [was] why, why didn't they go to war? Why didn't they fight and kill all the Germans? So, I was baffled, baffled that this had happened to our family and we weren't at war. I was angry, I felt a sense of shame that we had—that this had happened. Well, where were their guns?

Thus, Stephan incorporated early on not only a painful loss of identity, but also a specific quintessential Holocaust experience of shame and rage.

---

10 Five among the eighteen (twenty-seven percent), including Abby and Martha (see App. II); can this be a statistical anomaly? Examining the 2013 Pew Research Center's survey of American Jews, with its well-known somewhat controversial data on American Jewish intermarriage rates, I found no data relating to marriage patterns among converted Jewish families, perhaps further evidence of the largely unexplored nature of this demographic.

Like many of his cousins, he became obsessed with Jewish writers in high school. Later on, he had his first direct experience of antisemitism, a swastika defacing his dormitory room door at his liberal Catholic college, triggered, he believes, by his strong left-wing politics. His father's son, he settled the matter with fistfights.

Stephan has continued to actively grapple with his Jewish identity throughout his life.

> Under some definitions I'm not Jewish at all but under others Judaism is part of my core. I feel an affinity towards people who identity as being Jewish. I feel as though I have— I share something with them, I'm not exactly sure of what that is.

He acknowledges that these preoccupations strongly impacted his decision to marry a Jewish woman

> who practiced Judaism, whose family practiced Judaism, who had grown up with a kosher sink, kosher sinks, obviously, whose family said the *B'racha* over bread and wine, and lit candles. She'd gone to Hebrew school, she had a bat mitzvah, and she loved me and I loved her and we planned to have kids but that's not how things worked out.

Together they lived an active Jewish life. Steve especially loved Yom Kippur.

> And when it came time for, you know, the Day of Atonement and getting in touch with where am I not in sync with the ebb and flow of the universe and my relationships with others—that was the Jewish practice where I felt that I wasn't Other. When we did the other things I felt like I was being allowed to participate but I was actually supporting my wife in her practice.

After his marriage ended, Stephan entered into a serious relationship was with a secular Russian Jewish woman whose family had passed through Israel on their way to America. Together they had many discussions and arguments about what it meant to be Jewish. Stephan's current partner is also Jewish and secular. Together they seek out ways to honor the Jewish holidays. What is clear is that throughout his story, women take on the roles of generators and bearers of Jewish culture and structure and ground his inchoate, even conflicted sense of his own Jewish identity.

Jessica

In contrast, his sister Jessica is decisive.

> By the time I was five years old, I knew that I had Jewish family. Jewishness in the family
> history was around. My [non-Jewish] mother seemed to be most comfortable talking about
> Jewishness in the family and I knew my Oma, my great-grandmother, was Jewish. I was Jew-
> ish like I was a girl. I was Jewish like I was a sister. I was Jewish like I was—it had to do with
> identity. I grew up in a family that practiced the Roman Catholic faith, and so it was not
> Jewishness as a religion.

As an adult, Jessica married a Jewish man whose Judaism was only slightly less
attenuated than her own. Together they passed on to their three sons both Jewish
and Christian home rituals. The boys were circumcised "to be like Daddy" but
were not bar mitzvahed. The family had Seders, a mezuzah, a menorah, a Christmas tree, Easter egg hunts, but absolutely no religious practice. As adults, her
sons identify as Jewish if anything, never Christian, Jessica told me.

Jessica lived a far-flung life for two decades in Asia, South Asia, and Europe
with her journalist husband and their children. In Paris, she recalls,

> we lived in a courtyard, and if I heard people's heels on a courtyard, I would just think of
> jackboots. And they were strange experiences because they came out of some well of emo-
> tional response to a story that I didn't know I had such a profound response to.

We think again of Marianne Hirsch's concept of postmemory, inextricably linked
to both family and gender, reappearing again in full force in the third generation.
During the interview, Jessica broke into tears as she recalled hearing of her
grandmother's death.

> What welled up out of me was just—I just gave the east [i.e., Europe] the double finger and
> what I was feeling was, "fuck you motherfuckers, she died in her bed." It stayed with me for
> a couple of minutes. Triumph!

Jessica summarizes:

> I am Jew-ish. I am not a member of the Jewish faith and never have been. I am perfectly
> comfortable with the fact that there is also a Jewish people, and I am a member of the Jew-
> ish people. It's a fact of my existence. And I'm comfortable with it. Jewishness is, to me –
> there's that funny story of the fish—one fish turns to the other and goes, "What's water?"
> What's Jewish?

Debbie

Debbie presents a far more conflicted story. Raised by her Swiss Catholic mother (her father, my brother Andrew, died when she was in utero), Debbie understood herself to be Catholic. Her first contact with Jews was at her private girls school in Baltimore where, at one point, a classmate taunted her for not being Jewish. When Debbie, upset, recounted this incident to her uncle (and my brother) Philip, then a frequent family visitor, he exploded. "You have family that died in the Holocaust!" Debbie's response? "I had no idea, I did not know." Her mother's narrative of the Kuttner family was a Catholic one.

In high school Debbie began reading Jewish literature; in college, at McGill University attended years later by her cousin David, she enrolled in a Jewish Studies class only to drop it, intimidated by its "in-group" dynamics (shades of David!). She has kept all her Jewish Studies course books.

Debbie is very conscious of the fragmentation she has always experienced around her Jewish identity. She feels very marked by what she calls her "Jewish body," and cherishes a friend's note from Jerusalem: "I go into the old city and I see you everywhere." As an adult, Debbie grew closer to her Jewish identity through a former partner who, like Debbie, was Jewish through her father. Meeting at a radical lesbian book club, they soon began going together to a progressive synagogue. Although she defines herself as "'anti-organized religion," Debbie loved the synagogue and for a time became deeply immersed in Judaism.

> At first I felt like a total imposter. I know I look so Jewish and I'm walking in here acting like a Jew and I'm not part—I'm not joining this religion.

Nonetheless they began to observe the Jewish holidays together, got married in their synagogue, and planned to raise their children as Jews.

Once their children (a girl and a boy) arrived, however, a struggle began over what raising their children as Jews meant. To Debbie, it meant raising them within a Jewish ethical and moral order; to her partner it meant raising them in a fully observant Jewish household, a position that Debbie's lifelong, fierce anti-organized religious stance absolutely precluded. Their differences eventually became insurmountable and the couple divorced.

Today, Debbie's Jewish identity remains scattered (shards!) and deeply conflicted.

> I'm not Jewish because I'm not a practicing Jew. I've never been. I was not raised Jewish. I've never practiced the religion beyond doing it through my partner, with my partner, with my kids somewhat. At its heart, it's not who I am to be part of an organized religion. And so that is how I continue to completely identify as *I'm not Jewish* [italics added].

And later,

> I've always been fascinated with the Holocaust. It's my heritage. In that way, *I am Jewish* [italics added.] It's inside me. Even science is starting to explore the idea of maybe trauma is passed through genes—the trauma through Grandma, through my father, through me. It's in me.

Today Debbie routinely distributes her beloved grandma's "sort of autobiography" to her high school students as a teaching moment, reinforcing within her chosen profession her own link with the Holocaust and a public Jewish identity.

I would say that in her fragmented discursive style, in her vividly expressed, contradictory impulses about her identity ("I am Jewish"/"I am not Jewish"), Debbie embodies the extraordinary confusion, bordering on anguish, of cohabiting an essentially conflicted liminal space. (I am reminded once again of Rahel Varnhagen.) Debbie's preoccupation with her Jewish body, with her insider/outsider status, with what she experiences as "inherited trauma" in an obvious link to and embodiment of Marianne Hirsch's theories, are all markers in this complicated family story of the problematics and persistence of a post-conversion Jewish identity.

All three of my exemplars then, Stephan, Jessica, and Debbie, seem to have turned to Jewish partnerships or marriages to fill out an all-too-real, even urgent, if inchoate effort to grope their way out of the darkness and obscurity of an uncertain past. In the end it is only Martha, presented in Appendix II below, who is able to call herself "Judeo-Christian" without nuance or objection, on the surface at least at peace.

The Family as Jewish Culture

A striking number of my interviewees remark on their affinity with "Jewish culture." The way in which they use the term is notable: as an intellectual and principled tradition, strongly European, strongly cosmopolitan, strongly German Jewish then, and derived from family. Trying on being Jewish, finding a surprisingly comfortable fit, they fall into it almost gratefully as adults, almost with a sense of relief, almost in an "aha" moment, always, remarkably, as a sort of tribal recognition without any urgency to "join."

Nicholas K

Nick, brother of Steve and Jessica, blocked family origin stories, he says, until about the age of forty he says, when

> I realized the conversation about Jews included me in some way. I remember being shocked by that realization. All the illusions fell away and I was just left with "oh yeah, I guess I'm part Jewish." Not that long after that, somebody introduced me to this book about the impact of the Holocaust on the next generation after survivors. I was like "Oh yeah, I know these people." It was very understandable to me. That experience, that did affect my family. I can look at it and see that that's amazing. That looking at these people, these sort of recognizable characteristics, yeah, that's in my family too. The way in which things were said and not said. Things were talked about and not talked about.

In short, he grasped the silence and the shame underlying his own family's story. As for himself, Nick validates his strong cultural identification as a Jew, defined as

> an emphasis on intellectual things, and the value of knowledge and learning, and the importance of being an educated human being. Those, to me—that's central to it. So it all has to do, in some way, with what you value. That whether you're an academic or a professional, you're expected to learn and to use that learning. That, to me, is what I keep coming back to.

He also emphasizes

> another dimension of it, a tribal-like identity. I think between the intellectual dimension, what I see as being a European Jew, and the tribal identity of being a Jew. Those things are what I mostly think about as Jewish, or that I sort of just naturally seem to resonate with. The way I relate to other people, I automatically find it—I want to spend more time with people like that than I do, generally speaking, with people who aren't like that. It might not even be the individual, but there's just some sort of shared understanding. Again, it's like being a member, like a club. So you just automatically assume that person understands what you understand, knows what you know, appreciates what you appreciate —you have a shared understanding, which makes it easier to relate to.

Today:

> I actually will say I'm part Jewish. I don't say it often. It doesn't, I don't think, come up all that often in my life, but when it does that's how I self-identify. I never did that before. It never even occurred to me to do that before the age of forty. It's important to me in that I know it, because I feel like it's who I am.

Nick raised his two daughters in a secular household and did not tell them the family stories,

> but I will say it did not surprise me in the least that they both married Jews. On one hand, that's pure coincidence, but on the other I think it goes back to the sort of cultural—whatever cultural comfort zone they live in I think reflects, in part, mine.

Speaking of his eagerly anticipated first grandchild, due shortly after the interview:

> There will be a little girl named Lucy Rubenstein and her dad was bar mitzvahed and I'm pretty sure she'll be bat mitzvahed. I see that as entirely consistent with my existence in my family, and my life, and it seems a continuation of it.

His sense of calm, of peace, of acceptance, seems remarkable. Nick displays no urge to formally join a Jewish community or to embrace a Jewish religious identity or practice. And yet as he relates it, not only did he did come to a profound reckoning with his Holocaust history, he also recognized and fully embraced a inherent tribal identity, which to him is represented by shared values, a shared way of approaching the world. To Nick, this is the world of the European Jew replanted on new soil. His own abrupt conversion experience, if that's what we can call it, a self-created void abruptly transformed into self-knowledge and a strong sense of his place in the world, seems to sustain him, again outside the formal strictures of organized Judaism. His sisters Ann and Elizabeth, whose stories are featured in Appendix II, have flashes of Nick's insight, but without as sustained an impact.

Michele

Michele begins, "my father [my brother Andrew] died when I was only five and a half, and so my direct connection to the Jewish family was severed." Along with her siblings, Michele was raised as Catholic by her Swiss American Catholic mother. After her father's death, the family moved to Switzerland for several years, returning when Michele was in third grade.

Michele does not know when she found out that she had Jewish ancestry or if she had always known. "I knew that Grandma and Grandpa had been born Jewish but that they had switched to Catholic and so now we were all Catholic." At her private elementary girls school in Baltimore filled with affluent families, primarily Christian, some Jewish, she identified with the Jewish students as "Other." For Michele at that time, it was a Swiss Other, living in a Swiss home, eating Swiss food, celebrating Swiss holidays. Nonetheless, it is worth noting that she assumed the classical "Other" position, a position she identified as Jewish, while raised a Christian.

In high school, Michele regularly cared for a Jewish family's children and felt an immediate strong sense of kinship with the family grandmother, a German Jew. "Same accent, same vibrant character, loved music and the arts." This feeling of familiarity soon extended to the whole family; "these people are more like my people." Michele was beginning to understand, she says, that being Jewish was more than a religion. In school she learned about the Holocaust, read the Diary of Anne Frank and realized "Oh my gosh, that was part of my family!" And yet, her grandmother's Nazi escape stores were never scary to her. "Grandma was always positive. She never dwelled on the negative." It was only much later that she realized that actual family members had been murdered in the Holocaust.

The turning point for Michele's Jewish identity came in her late twenties, when she became close to her then cousin-in-law, Stephan K's first wife.

> She was the first Jewish person who identified me as a Jew. And she thought of me as one of her tribe. And I was fascinated. We had many conversations. When she said that we [the Kuttners] were really a big Jewish family, I started to think about it and notice it.

And so Michele began to try on thinking of herself as Jewish, complicated for her by the fact that she was Jewish through her long-deceased father.

Today, Michele openly and comfortably identifies as half-Jewish, careful only to specify "not religious at all." She and her husband did not raise their two children in any religious tradition, and yet after they were born, her feeling of vulnerability, a vulnerability I tie to her Holocaust heritage, increased. "And so then I began to own more that, in fact this is something [she emphasizes the word], to be Jewish." Michele's children know they are Jewish, Michele says, even though she never developed a conscious narrative with them on this issue. She has many Jewish and what she calls half-Jewish friends and regularly gets invited to Seders and Yom Kippur break-fasts, although, she "sort of feels like a fake."

Here is how Michele feels Jewish today. Jewish men feel very familiar and comfortable to her, reminding her of her uncles. "It's just being like. Similar. It must be a way of looking at life." She sees herself as having adopted what she sees as Jewish culture from her grandparents.

> There's a certain Jewish culture that I think my grandparents absorbed in their families growing up. And they, together, passed it on to your generation. So you guys retained that culture. I don't know what it is. Maybe there's a warmth to it. There's a warmth and

a love of the creative arts. Even if my grandparents were Catholics, I think they did it in a Jewish way. There were foods, there were songs, the music. And I find that comfortable and familiar.

Michele, with her red hair and blue eyes, has been exposed to a sort of casual antisemitism by people who are unaware that she is Jewish. "And then we [herself and her daughter, who resembles her] have to say, 'actually, we're part of them' or 'but you're talking about me!'" In pride of place in Michele's living room hangs a copy of a family painting of four eighteenth-century paternal ancestors, brothers. Michele always felt an affinity to these ancestors because of their red hair, but, startlingly, only realized in the course of her interview that they were of course Jews!

Thus, Michele has come to feel deeply Jewish through her family: her father, her ex-sister-in-law, her uncles, her grandparents, and, ironically, through a Jewish body type she only recently has understood to include her, linkages she experiences as both broadly cultural and deeply comforting. Issues of religion concern her not a whit.

Lisa

Lisa, my sister Barbara's daughter, recalls no defining moment of learning that she had a Jewish heritage. She did realize that she was somehow Jewish as a teen, but like her cousin Abby felt like "an outsider" to the large Jewish community in Berkeley. As an adult, Lisa proudly claims her Jewish Outsider status. She believes it grew out of her awareness of what she sees as her Jewish body—her dramatic dark coloring, her thick curly hair—traits she shares with her mother, who is and was uncomfortable with a perceived Jewish body according to Lisa. She was raised with no religion, although her family celebrated and continues to celebrate Christmas.

Today, Lisa sees herself as part of what she calls a "cultural Jewish heritage," which she identifies with "the way grandma and grandpa lived their lives, even though they were practicing Catholics." To Lisa, this means a way of life she sees as "stressing the value of education, music and learning," and a heritage that she identifies as "very European, also very Jewish, an intellectual sort of lifestyle." To Lisa, this heritage "is so embedded in me that it's also who I am and a really strong part of my identity." In fact, "I do say I am Jewish." She remains quick to specify, when voicing that identity, that her Judaism is not at all religious and that she is not interested in Judaism's religious aspects. Although her mother does not identify as Jewish, Lisa believes that Judaism comes through the maternal line. "I feel Jewish; I don't feel Catholic (her father's background)."

Lisa retains vivid memories of her grandmother's Nazi escape stories and always knew that "the family story was tied to a real, concrete history in the very recent past." Like so many of the third generation, she especially remembers "the prostitute" in a story that seemed almost magical, summed up as "Can you believe it? I knew a prostitute and she saved my life!" With keen analytical insight, she sees her grandmother as "a Jewish woman who found a way to deal with the horror through these narratives she would tell. She shaped and reshaped the story so that you didn't get a sense of the fear. The reality of the story is absolutely terrifying, and that's not the way she ever told the story." In other words, Lisa grasps the concept of authorship, of her grandmother's narrative as a conscious tool, both for herself and for the many children and grandchildren to whom she taught her truth, her *Jewish* truth, in a tale that mirrored, all unconsciously, that age-old Jewish trope, the journey from oppression to freedom.

To summarize, in each of the three narratives above, then, we find a growing identification with a highly European, secular Judaism, closely tied to the German Jewish values we know today as *Bildung*, centered in learning and in education, in self-knowledge arrived at through story. The People of the Book.

The Challenge of the Jewish Holidays

In 2014, my brother Tom, in Berkeley for a sabbatical, organized a Bay Area Kuttner family Seder. Just about all of us locals were there, perhaps twenty or so, as Tom led us through the Elie Wiesel Haggadah while we feasted on traditional foods. It was the first time our family had celebrated Passover together in over a hundred years. I begin then, with the stories of two of Tom's children, for whom a primary connection with Judaism, unlike the rest of us, was through a Jewish holiday ritual.

Stephanie

Like her younger brothers Ben and David, Stephanie's initial and only exposure to Judaism was what she learned from her father in the context of the Jewish holidays. As all three relate, their local and only synagogue in their small Canadian college town was Orthodox. That *schul*, unfortunately, absolutely refused to recognized the family as Jewish. As a result, "our Judaism was very secular. We recognized and celebrated the Jewish holidays, generally on our own, or with family friends." The repercussion of this narrow Jewish gatekeeping affected the contours of their subsequent Jewish lives.

As a young adult, Stephanie went to Oxford as a Rhodes Scholar. There she soon adopted an identity as a proud Jewish feminist, and began attending meetings on Friday evenings with other Jewish students.

> And in a very open way, we called it "the minyan." It was potluck. Someone would take responsibility for hosting, and picking a topic, sometimes background information, for discussion. And this is exactly the kind of Judaism that was of interest to me. I always say I became more Jewish and more feminist by going to Oxford University.

Stephanie's boyfriend (now husband), a secular Swedish Lutheran, shared her interest in world cultures and religions and attended the minyan with her. To this day Stephanie feels that "my closest friends in life are primarily people that we knew at Oxford University." Her work there became focused on the growing field of gender-based human rights violations. She attributes her lifelong professional involvement with minority rights as "very much tied to, first of all, my father and his trajectory and an understanding of being part of a minority that has suffered some of the most horrific annihilation violence." After Oxford, Stephanie and her husband's joint professional lives unfolded in the world of multinational organizations in Mozambique, Haiti, Laos, Brazil, and elsewhere, with stints in New York and Washington, D.C.

Stephanie's Jewish life has always centered exclusively on her circle of family and friends and consists almost entirely of Shabbat and other holiday dinners. She and her husband agreed to circumcise their son and to raise both their children with a variety of cultural influences while inculcating them in a form of Jewish identity.

> It's never been a question that, in my family, and in the entire Kuttner family, we are Jews. And some had left Judaism, or left the religious community of Judaism. But it was never—it was never a question. It was just who we were. So we were Jews. We agreed that it would be important to transfer our various family histories, family cultures. Since they've [the children] been born, we have tried every year to do Passover and Hanukkah, because we've lived around the world. We've been in Laos, and we've been in Brasilia, neither of which has a strong Jewish community. So we just would invite friends to do Hanukkah, to do Passover. It requires of me a fair amount of—it's up to me to actually figure out what these *stories* [italics added] are. That's why I have a feminist Haggadah, a kid's Haggadah, a humanist Haggadah, because I don't have a lot of religious education. But as you know, the ceremonies are storytelling around which there are some ideas. So we like to talk about that with the kids. And I have books about Hanukkah, and I have books about Passover. They also have a Christmas tree and hang a Star of David decorations among others.

Ultimately, Stephanie sees Judaism and Jewish identity as a cultural and historical phenomenon, passed down through storytelling. She is absolutely clear that her strong personal and professional investment in issues of gender and genocide is strongly rooted in Jewish history and experience. Like her father, her Judaism is largely family-based and unaffiliated, an identity that she has passed on to her children as part of the multicultural fabric of their family life and experience. She remains fiercely and unapologetically secular, rejecting "religion" as invariably misogynistic and hierarchical, and gravitating towards Buddhism for her spiritual expression. In a close reflection of her father's thinking, Stephanie sums up her position on Judaism as follows:

> I think the Jewish identity is an element of this bigger moral education that I believe in, or that is part of my identity, and that I think is so critical and empowering to pass on to children. Judaism as an ethical system. I find it's deeply important to me to transfer that to my children. Not as their only identity, but as an element of their identity. Because that is a central element of our family's identity and history, even if whether or not parts of our Kuttner family decide to practice Catholicism and don't necessarily themselves identify with Judaism. I already explained to my children in terms that they can understand, they know about the Holocaust, they know that our grandparents were lucky to survive. These sorts of things still happen. This is what's so relevant to me. I talk to them about that. I think the Jewish identity is an element of this bigger moral education that I believe in, or that is part of my identity, and that I think is so critical and empowering to pass on to the children.

Ben

Ben too recalls a childhood marked by his father's strong Jewish influence.

> My father really made efforts to make us aware of our heritage and what is the significance and importance of the various holidays. As a kid, I looked forward to Hanukkah because of the gifts. I have fond memories of Passovers. We would read the Haggadah, and that story was a cornerstone of my Jewish identity, the idea of a people oppressed and suppressed, and the Exodus from Egypt and arriving in a better place. Because we weren't going to services and we weren't listening to other people talk about Judaism, that became such an important part of my young Jewish identity.

Ben felt isolated as a Jew in Fredericton,

> because my mother's originally not Jewish, and her conversion wasn't recognized by the Jewish community where we grew up. I felt kind of alone in a lot of ways, because I knew that we were a Jewish family [and] celebrated Hanukkah and Passover as opposed to Christmas and Easter. But we didn't do anything with a larger community group.

All that changed when at age eighteen Ben enrolled in a yearlong international student program at Beersheba's Ben-Gurion University in conjunction with his father's sabbatical in Jerusalem. Not surprisingly, Ben's eleven-month stay in Israel had a decisive impact on his Jewish identity, one that was nuanced and multidirectional. His overall conclusion: "If I had not gone to Israel, I would not have the same feeling of connectedness to my Jewish heritage."

> For the first time in my life, I was surrounded by Jews. It was a very, very different experience than I'd had growing up to that point. Interestingly enough, that experience was also a little bit isolating, because despite being in the company of all of these Jews, there were a lot of people that I met and grew to know in Israel who didn't really consider me to be a Jew either. Growing up apart and away from anybody else to identify with and being surrounded by the Jewish tradition and religion but not feeling entirely one hundred percent welcome there, either. That's the time for me that I feel like I developed my own religious identity outside of the cocoon of my upbringing and my family. And I think what I decided—and I did decide—that it was very important to me [to] self-identify as being Jewish. I never felt obliged in any sense to be more religious in a traditional sense. But I've always felt, and especially going through young adulthood, now raising my own family, that it's really important to recognize our heritage.

During his time in Israel, Ben became quite friendly with the owners of a local restaurant-bar where he worked. This French-speaking Moroccan couple often invited him to their large family Shabbat dinners where everyone spoke French[11] and shared with him their way of practicing Judaism. Among his fellow students, an international group in which he nevertheless felt very included despite their occasional reservations ("it was almost unspoken that there was the Jewish thing that tied us"), there were many conversations about religion and identity. In all these experiences, Ben says, "I was, for the first time, seeing a spectrum of how people view and interpret Jewishness. And that was striking to me." He also became acutely aware of an Israeli "subculture of hatred," recalling what do him were traumatic experiences around the issue of Palestine that "more than anything else gave me much deeper appreciation for the complexity of the Jewish identity [in] Israel—and turned me off frankly." To Ben, these experiences formed part of his new understanding of the wide range of Jewishness.

Returning back to New Brunswick, Ben left the family home and stopped celebrating the Jewish holidays, instead joining his girlfriend Tanya in her family's Christmas celebrations. Nonetheless, the couple eventually got married under a *chuppah* in a "not overly religious" Jewish ceremony jointly written by Ben and his father Tom, who presided. Together, the couple agreed to keep some of the

---

11 Ben, like his siblings, attended bilingual public schools in Canada and is fluent in French.

Jewish traditions he had grown up with. He relates the story of their son's medical circumcision, paid for out of pocket.

> [It was] a pretty intense experience. I felt really torn hearing him cry. Tanya just didn't want to be part. I took Emmanuel to a different part of the hospital. The doctor came and performed the circumcision. And then I carried Emmanuel back to his mom. And it was important because I have so little to latch onto in a sense. I don't have a history of deep cultural exposure to draw on. So I'm being very candid in saying that at least with the circumcision, I got that one down. And it'll maybe be the cornerstone of things to come.

The family began celebrating Hanukkah after their son turned three. Ben bought him children's Hanukkah books as "little ways of exposure and trying to build understanding. And I think inevitably, I model some of what I hope to be doing with him on my experience." Ben is very proud that his son Emmanuel, age seven at the time of our interview, identifies as Jewish, recounting with gusto how his son came home from school recently with "Hey, Dad, you know, Isaac's a Jew, too!"

In short, like Stephanie, Ben's Jewish story highlights the strong and decisive influence of his father. He consciously is raising his son as a Jew along the same model, emphasizing "the important linkages between our family's history and the Jewish tradition." Like Tom, Ben has no contact with any Jewish communal organizations in Toronto where he now lives. While his relationship to his grandmother's Jewish story resonates, ("I think that it's really important to me personally to trace my identity through that experience"), his own Jewish narrative is a story of father-to-son transmission, a pattern that he saw in his father's own experience, and one he is committed to with his son. Again like Tom, his Israeli experience decisively cemented his Jewish identity.

Myself

Circling back to the beginning of this book, I end this last chapter with my own reflections on the Jewish holidays, a prism for both the estrangement and the lure of a ritual past. A memory surfaces—my very first visit to a synagogue, an adult groping her way back to Judaism. That evening, I had somehow found my way to a small Reconstructionist *kehilla* in Berkeley, California on what I now know to call *erev* Yom Kippur. Slipping into a pew, bathed in the dying light of a gorgeous California sunset, my senses absorbed in the unfamiliar chants and melodies in an unknown language, I experienced an almost overpowering wave of connection to an ancient past, a past I could finally claim in that instant. It was for me a pivotal moment. The feeling of euphoria faded, however, as over the succeeding years I gingerly stepped into the occasional open community Seder, feeling lost, feeling alienated, feeling the deep ache of the stranger in a strange land. All was new, all was unfamiliar, and I didn't know how I would ever belong.

Eventually I did find a way to come in, to find my place, to openly acknowledge to my new friends my checkered past, my Catholic girlhood, the many baptisms, and begin to take in their acceptance. And yet, and yet. Despite my current active synagogue involvement, a master's degree in Jewish History and Culture under my belt, the hard-won completion of this very book project, I still experience each year the old anguish, the old wound, of the Jewish holidays. Not in the services—without fail I love them as unreservedly as I did that very first time when I fell in love with a Judaism I had never known. It is the holiday dinners at Rosh Hashanah, after Yom Kippur, at the springtime Seders, amidst the unrestrained joy in familiar rituals and foods and fellowship, everyone awash in nostalgia and love and family—it is then that I feel most keenly my distance and my pain. In truth, my own joyful holiday memories go back to the Christmases of my childhood, to a time when our family really worked, when our love for one another spilled out amid the sharp scent of pine and the blaze of flickering candlelight, in the familiar foods (including, as I discovered later, many an Ashkenazic treat). So yes, I have learned the vocabulary of brisket, of apple and honey, of challah, of *matzah* and *charoset*, the cadences of progressive and traditional Haggadot. But all these are not really my language, my cherished memories, my nostalgia, and so I find myself once again outside the magic circle I so longed to enter. Their reminiscences, steeped in the *Yiddishkeit* of a lost Eastern European world, are not my reminiscences. Their *Pesach* songs are not my songs, the Christmas carols we played around the piano on many a festive Christmas eve, my father, the musician, brilliantly riffing his way through the familiar melodies celebrating a wondrous birth, we all lustily joining in, my mother's clear soprano rising above us like the evening star itself. Yes, I have learned the new ways, but they are not always my ways. So the Jewish family holidays invariably mark for me a space of not belonging, of doubleness, the space of the outsider, belonging neither here nor there, throwing me back to our uncertain beginnings, to my mother's story. And yet her story so strongly carries within itself the seeds of a powerful healing, a Jewish healing, the possibility of return, *teshuvah*, to which this book serves as testament (I use the term advisedly), as testimony. For it is in story, her story and ours, that we have found our lost Jewish selves in what I argue is a particularly Jewish way. So for me, at this year's 2020 Yom Kippur service, a virtual one to be sure in the midst of pestilence and other previously unimaginable threats, flooded with feeling, I got to experience a sense of deepest joy, and yes, belonging, at being reunited with my people in chant, in song, at being called upon, once again, to choose life. As my mother so invariably did. And so a fitting end piece to my own frontispiece, my Preface, its mysterious ambiguities resolved for me at last, at this time, in this space.

Reflections

We may grow weary of these many stories. And yet, in the diversity of responses and the almost bewildering array of options chosen by this third generation as to their inherited Jewish identity, presented both here and below in Appendix II, perhaps the most gratifying impulse to me among almost all of these many voices has been the strength, indeed the persistence of a Jewish commitment, however defined. No matter how distant from a traditional Jewish paradigm, that commitment almost invariably has been manifested in a serious and active grappling with a complex Jewish heritage and an acknowledgement of how important it is. While the Holocaust and its extreme violent Jewish naming from without looms large, frequently with traumatic resonance, it is ultimately the strong impact of the internal Jewish naming, the impact of the storyteller, the religious scholar, and the German Jewish culture they personified, that made the difference in each of my narrators' journey of self-discovery. For me then, my book bears witness, among other things, to the concept of Judaism as ultimately a family affair, reinforced by the gaze of the Other.

This book bears witness as well to the concept of Judaism as a journey, a journey of change, of transformation, the journey of a people on the move. Here, together then, we have traveled down that long and winding road, the road of my family's Jewish journey, the road of Judaism itself, of destruction and loss and renewal, the journey of constant return. As in my brother's photograph of the hot and dusty road to Theresienstadt that graces the cover of this book, its trees an exclamation point, a road to death becomes a road to renewal in this our family story.

Conclusion

When I first undertook this project, I felt determined to have my converted parents' descendants, my siblings and our offspring, *know* that they were Jewish, determined to initiate a process in which we together recovered our common Judaism. As it turned out, they all did the work for me. One after another, they each wrote their own idiosyncratic Jewish selves into being through their own words in many a moving interview. At first, I felt elated. I felt I had succeeded in single-handedly reconstituting our own Lost Jewish Tribe. And to some extent, that was true. And yet, as time went on and I reflected on everything everyone had said, I felt the dark side of our collective story, its obverse, the huge *lostness* of our Lost Jewish Tribe. How often I heard some variant of the phrase, "I know I'm Jewish, but I don't know anything about it." And in many cases, my interviewees were right; they really knew very little about Judaism in all its immense cultural, religious, philosophical, and historical richness. Some of us, among them myself obviously, have sought to remedy these gaps; others not so much.

A second significant loss runs through these many stories—the loss of community, and the many fumbling, makeshift attempts to make up for it. It is in this vein that I see the frequent if indirect or even covert claims of Membership in the Tribe, *our* Tribe, however expressed.

What then are we to make of this Lost Tribe, my family? Obviously the Holocaust, its actuality and its mythos in terms of the family narrative, plays a huge role. Second in importance, but by no means insignificant, is the impact of a strongly felt and cherished cultural affinity with the world of the German Jew. And we cannot forget the impact of gender that permeates these many stories: the matriarch, originator of the story that is itself a replay of a very old Jewish story, myself, the gatherer of stories, the many emergent motifs of women as bearers of culture, the lure of matrilineal descent, all calling out to the many grandchildren.

And so I move beyond the concept of loss "to the performativity and narrativity of the Jewish text" in Leslie Morris's evocative words that so perfectly capture the thrust of my own project.[1] Indeed, Morris's very title, *The Translated Jew*, forces a renewed focus on the whole issue of translation as central to the entire Jewish project, illuminated by Benjamin's gnomic (and revolutionary) assertion of translation as the "afterlife" of a text.[2] Commenting on Benjamin and his priv-

---

1 Morris, 8.
2 Walter Benjamin, "The Task of the Translator," in Lawrence Venuti, ed., *The Translation Studies Reader* (New York: Routledge, 2000) 15–25, 16.

https://doi.org/10.1515/9783110731965-011

ileging of translation as transformation and renewal, Naomi Seidman, rejecting like Benjamin the "rhetoric of loss," insists instead on a vision of Jewish culture that "emerges as a continual translation and transformation."[3] For me, then, envisioning my family texts here as translation narratives, I elevate them, as Seidman suggests, to the level of "autobiographic allegory, stories that represent identity as split, multiple, or shifting."[4]

It follows then that, revisiting Benjamin's epigram that I situate at the head of my Introduction, ("In the fields with which we are concerned, knowledge comes only in lightning flashes. The text is the long roll of thunder that follows."[5]), I am also drawn to Morris's conceit of the shards of the past that "come together in a flash with the now to form a constellation." Within this formulation, she opines, "the roll of thunder is the movement into the future, carrying the flash of knowledge and insight."[6] This then is my project. History as montage, as Benjamin puts it elsewhere.[7] The kabbalistic notion of shards or points of light that surfaces so frequently in my own commentary on my many (translation) narratives then become constitutive of the fragmentation of the German Jewish experience, markers of the restlessness and the drive toward mutability unleashed in modernity, prefigured in Rahel Varnhagen's story. It is telling to me that Seyla Benhabib, in her book on conceptions of history among German Jewish intellectuals in exile, instructs us that "for Arendt [and we remember her here as noted biographer of Rahel Varnhagen], honest thinking can only be accomplished in fragments" in what Benhabib terms her "Benjaminian moment;" indeed, Benhabib summarizes with the phrase "fragmentary constellations."[8]

Which brings me to the issue of diaspora identity. Daniel and Jonathan Boyarin, in their provocative 1993 article "Diaspora: Generation and the Ground of Jewish Identity," controversially privilege diaspora over the Jewish nationalist enterprise as a richer, more authentic source of historical Jewish identity.[9] Cynthia Baker for her part takes up the Boyarin claims that "disasporic identity is a disaggregated identity" and that "Jewishness disrupts the very categories of

3 Seidman, *Faithful Renderings*, 10.

4 Ibid., 7.

5 Benjamin, *Arcades*, 456.

6 Morris, 17, citing Sigrid Weigel. See ibid., 203, note 47. The originary language however is pure Benjamin. "Image is that wherein what has been comes together in a flash in the now to form a constellation." Benjamin, *Arcades*, 462.

7 Benjamin, *Arcades*, 461.

8 Seyla Benhabib, *Exile, Statelessness, and Migration: Playing Chess with History from Hannah Arendt to Isaiah Berlin* (Princeton University Press, 2018), 36.

9 See Daniel Boyarin, Jonathan Boyarin, "Diaspora: Generation and the Ground of Jewish Identity." *Critical Inquiry* 19, no. 4 (Summer 1993): 693–725.

identity," to argue that "all modes of identification are 'mixed,' interdependent, partial, and contingent,' and stand 'in dialectical tension with one another.'"[10] It is for this reason that I argue that the extreme diasporic modality represented by conversion actually falls within the Jewish enterprise, albeit at its margins. And so I locate my family of diaspora Jews whom we have visited here, born of refugees themselves of fragmented identity, scattered among many cities, states, countries, and continents, at the center of an ongoing exploration of what it means to be Jewish; indeed, what it means to write a Jewish text.

In conclusion therefore I return with Benjamin, brilliant theorist of modernity, prophet of postmodernity, to the concept of translation as the afterlife of a text. Here in my book the text is Judaism itself, born as story, born as family. Finally we come back to genealogy, to story, to the story of a family, as in our original sources, as in the Five Books of Moses. My mother as translator, evoking the shards of the entire German Jewish experience in her insistent repeated messages to us all to remember our origins, to remember and honor our mythic and miraculous flight from oppression, from annihilation to freedom, "your family history." And our own stories as translations again of her text, circling around the conundrum of what it means to live as a Jew in the world, "not Judaism as a religious, civilizational, or national entity, 'essence' or system, but of the perception of realty through ... the experience of being a 'Jew in the world.'"[11] It seems that one by one, each of us has found ourselves compelled in one way or another to walk on that path, to experience ourselves as Jews and to embrace that identity, mostly willingly, with a sense of relief, more rarely unwillingly, in all its beautiful, "split, multiple, and shifting" manifestations. Our own beautiful fragmentary constellation.

---

10 Baker, 128, Internal citations are to Daniel and Jonathan Boyarin, 721.
11 Dan Miron, *From Continuity to Contiguity* (Stanford: Stanford University Press, 2010), 306–307, cited in Morris, 12.

Bibliography

Amishai-Maisels, Ziva. "Chagall's 'White Crucifixion.'" *Art Institute of Chicago Museum Studies* 17, no. 2 (1991): 139–181. DOI:10.2307/4101588

Arendt, Hannah. *Rahel Varnhagen: The Life of a Jewess*. Edited by Liliane Weissberg. Translated by Richard and Clara Winston. Baltimore: The Johns Hopkins University Press, 1907.

Baer, Yizhak. *History of the Jews in Christian Spain*. 2 vols. Philadelphia: Jewish Publication Society of America, 1966.

Baker, Cynthia M. *Jew*. New Brunswick: Rutgers University Press, 2016.

Baron, Salo. *A Social and Religious History of the Jews*. 2nd ed. Vol. 15. New York: Columbia University Press, 1973.

Benhabib, Seyla. *Exile, Statelessness, and Migration: Playing Chess with History from Hannah Arendt to Isaiah Berlin*. Princeton University Press, 2018.

Benjamin, Walter. *The Arcades Project*. Translated by Howard Eiland and Kevin McLaughlin. Cambridge: Belknap, 1999.

Benjamin, Walter. "The Task of the Translator." Edited by Lawrence Venuti. *The Translation Studies Reader*. New York: Routledge, 2000, 14–25.

Biale, David. *Not In the Heavens: The Tradition of Jewish Secular Thought*. Princeton: Princeton University Press, 2011.

Bodian, Miriam. *Hebrews of the Portuguese Nation*. Bloomington: Indiana University Press, 1997.

Borges, Jorge Luis. "Kafka and His Precursors." *Labyrinths*. Translated by James E. Irby. New York: New Directions Publishing Corporation, 2007.

Botelho, Angela. "Modern Marranism and the German-Jewish Experience: The Persistence of Jewish Identity in Conversion." Master's Thesis, Graduate Theological Union, Berkeley California, 2013.

Botelho, Angela. "The Marrano in Modernity: The Case of Karl Gutzkow." In *Nexus* 3, 123–143. Rochester: Camden House Press, 2017.

Boyarin, Daniel, and Boyarin, Jonathan. "Diaspora: Generation and the Ground of Jewish Identity." *Critical Inquiry* 19, no. 4 (Summer 1993): 693–725.

Cohen, Shaye J. D. *The Beginnings of Jewishness: Boundaries, Varieties, Uncertainties* Berkeley: University of California Press, 1999.

Da Costa, Uriel. *A Specimen of Human Life*. New York: Bergman Publishers, 1967.

Derrida, Jacques. *Archive Fever: A Freudian Impression*. Translated by Eric Prenowitz. Chicago: University of Chicago Press, 1996.

Derrida, Jacques. *Judeities: Questions for Jacques Derrida*. Edited by Bettina Bergo, Joseph Cohen, and Raphael Zagury-Orley. Translated by Bettina Bergo and Michael B. Smith. New York: Fordham University Press, 2007.

Deutscher, Ivan. *The Non-Jewish Jew and Other Essays*. New York: Verso, 2017.

Efron, John M. *German Jewry and the Allure of the Sephardic*. Princeton: Princeton University Press, 2016.

Elon, Amos. *The Pity of It All: A Portrait of Jews in Germany, 1743–1933*. New York: Henry Holt and Company, 2002.

Endelman, Todd. *Leaving the Jewish Fold: Conversion and Radical Assimilation in Modern Jewish History*. Princeton: Princeton University Press, 2015.

https://doi.org/10.1515/9783110731965-012

Endelman, Todd. "Welcoming Ex-Jews in the Jewish Historiographical Fold." *The Margins of Jewish History*. Edited by Marc Lee Raphael. Williamsburg, VA: Department of Religion, The College of William and Mary, 2000.

Fremont, Helen. *After Long Silence*. New York: Delacorte, 1999.

Friedländer, Saul. *The Years of Persecution*. Vol. 1. *Nazi German and the Jews*. New York: HarperCollins, 1997.

Friedländer, Saul. *The Years of Extermination*. Vol. 2. *Nazi German and the Jews*. New York: HarperCollins, 2007.

Glatzer, Nahum N. *Franz Rosenzweig: His Life and Thought*. New York: Farrar, Straus and Young, 1953.

Gutzkow, Karl. *Uriel Acosta: In Three Acts*. Translated by Henry Spicer. London: Kegan Paul, Trench: 1885.

Halberstam, Chaya. "Wisdom, *Torah*, Nomos: The Discursive Contours of Biblical Law." Law, Culture, and the Humanities 9: no. 1 (2013): 50–58. http://journals.sagepub.com/doi/10.1177/1743872111404174.

Fremont, Helen. *After Long Silence: A Memoir*. New York: Delacorte, 1999.

Hertz, Deborah. *How Jews Became Germans: The History of Conversion and Assimilation in Berlin*. New Haven: Yale University Press, 2007.

Hertz Deborah. *Jewish High Society in Old Regime Berlin*. Syracuse: Syracuse University Press, 2005.

Hirsch, Marianne. *Family Frames: Photography, Narrative, and Postmemory*. (Cambridge, MA: Harvard University Press, 1997).

Hirsch, Marianne. "The Generation of Postmemory." *Poetics Today* 29, no. 1 (Spring 2008): 103–128.

Hirsch, Marianne. *The Generation of Postmemory: Writing and Visual Culture After the Holocaust*. New York: Columbia University Press, 2012.

Hoffman, Eva. *After Such Knowledge: Memory, History, and the Legacy of the Holocaust*. New York: Public Affairs, 2004.

Hyman, Paula E. *Gender and Assimilation in Modern Jewish History*. Seattle: University of Washington Press, 1995.

Jonte-Pace, Diane. "When Throne and Altar Are in Danger: Freud, Mourning, and Religion in Modernity." *Disciplining Freud on Religion*. Edited by Gregory Kaplan and William B. Parsons. New York: Lexington Books, 2010.

Kafka, Franz. *Letters to Malena*. Translated by Phillip Boehm. New York: Schocken, 1990.

Kaplan, Marion A. *The Making of the Jewish Middle Class: Women, Family, and Identity in Imperial Germany*. Oxford: Oxford University Press, 1991.

Kaplan, Marion A. "Unter Uns: Jews Socializing with other Jews in Imperial Germany." *Leo Baeck Institute Yearbook* 48 (2003): 41–65.

Kuttner, Stephan. *The History of Ideas and Doctrines of Canon Law in the Middle Ages*. London: Variorum Reprints, 1980.

Kuttner, Thomas S. "Stephan Kuttner: Both German Jew and Catholic Scholar." *Journal of Law, Philosophy and Culture* 5, no. 1 (Spring 2010): 43–65.

The Life of Glückel of Hameln: A Memoir. Translated and edited by Beth-Zion Abrahams. Philadelphia: The Jewish Publication Society, 2010.

Lowenstein, Steven M. *The Berlin Jewish Community: Enlightenment, Family and Crisis, 1770–1830*. New York: Oxford University Press, 1994.

Marks, Elaine. *Marrano as Metaphor: The Jewish Presence in French Writing*. New York: Columbia University Press, 1996.

Mendes-Flohr, Paul. *Divided Passions: Jewish Intellectuals and the Experience of Modernity*. Detroit: Wayne State University Press, 1990.

Mendes-Flohr, Paul. *German Jews: A Dual Identity*. New Haven: Yale University Press, 1999.

Meyer, Michael A. *Jewish Identity in the Modern World*. London: University of London Press, 1990.

Meyer, Michael A. *Judaism Within Modernity: Essays on Jewish History and Religion*. Detroit: Wayne State University Press, 2001.

Miron, Dan. *From Continuity to Contiguity*. Stanford: Stanford University Press, 2010.

Morris, Leslie. "Postmemory, Postmemoir." *Unlikely History: The Changing German-Jewish Symbiosis, 1945–2000*, 291–306. Edited by Leslie Morris and Jack Zipes. New York: Palgrave, 2002.

Morris, Leslie. *The Translated Jew*. Evanston: Northwestern University Press, 2018.

Mosse, George L. *German Jews Beyond Judaism*. Bloomington: Indiana University Press, 1984.

Mosse, Werner E. *The German–Jewish Economic Elite, 1820–1935: A Socio-Cultural Profile*. New York: Oxford University Press, 1989.

Mufti, Aamir. *Enlightenment in the Colony: The Jewish Question and the Crisis of Post-Colonial Culture*. Princeton: Princeton University Press, 2007.

Myers, David N. *Resisting History*. Princeton: Princeton University Press, 2003.

Phillips, Adam, ed. *The Penguin Freud Reader*. Translated by Shaun Whiteside. London: Penguin Classics, 2006.

Presner, Todd Samuel. *Muscular Judaism: The Jewish Body and the Politics of Regeneration*. New York: Routledge, 2007.

Radstone, Susannah, and Bill Schwartz, eds. *Memory: Histories, Theories, Debates*. New York: Fordham University Press, 2010.

Raphael, Melissa. "Goddess Religion, Postmodern Jewish Feminism, and the Complexity of Alternative Religious Identities." *Nova Religio: The Journal of Alternative and Emergent Religions* 1:2 (1998), 198–215.

Reszke, Katya. *Return of the Jew*. Boston: Academic Studies Press, 2013.

Roth, Cecil. *A History of the Marrano* . 4th ed. New York: Harmon Press, 1974.

Seidman, Naomi. *Faithful Renderings*. Chicago: The University of Chicago Press, 2006.

Seidman, Naomi. "Jewish Identity as a Psychic Wound." *The Marginalia Review of Books*. June 19, 2017. https://marginalia.lareviewofbooks.org/jewish-identity-psychic-wound/

Schainker, Ellie R. *Confessions of the Shtetl: Converts from Judaism in Imperial Russia, 1817–1906*. Stanford: Stanford University Press, 2016.

Shandler, Jeffrey. *Holocaust Memory in the Digital Age: Survivors' Stories and the New Media Practices*. Stanford: Stanford University Press, 2017.

Schmugge, Ludwig. "Stephan Kuttner (1907–1996) the 'Pope' of Canon Law Studies Between Germany, the Vatican and the USA." Translated by Michael Kuttner. *Bulletin of Medieval Canon Law* 30 (2013): 141–165.

Schorsch, Ismar. "The Myth of Sephardic Supremacy." *Leo Baeck Institute Yearbook* 14 (1989): 47–66.

Skolnick, Jonathan. *Jewish Pasts, German Fictions: History, Memory, and Minority Culture in Germany, 1824–1955*. Stanford: Stanford University Press, 2014.

Sorkin, David. *The Transformation of German Jewry: 1780–1840*. Detroit: Wayne State University Press, 1999.

Steinberg, Michael P. *Judaism Musical and Unmusical*. Chicago: University of Chicago Press, 2007.

Van Loon, Hendrick. *The Story of the Bible*. New York: Boni & Liveright, 1923.

Wullschläger, Jackie. *Chagall*. New York, Alfred A. Knopf, 2008.

Yovel, Yirmiyahu. *Spinoza and Other Heretics: The Marrano of Reason*. Princeton: Princeton University Press, 1989.

Yovel, Yirmiyahu. *The Other Within*. Princeton: Princeton University Press, 2009.

Yerushalmi, Yosef. *Freud's Moses: Judaism Terminable and Interminable*. New Haven: Yale University Press, 1991.

Yerushalmi, Yosef. *From Spanish Court to Italian Ghetto*. Seattle: University of Washington Press, 1971.

Appendix I
Eva Kuttner's "Sort of Autobiography"

I include here the actual typewritten text of my mother's 1998 "sort of autobiography," laboriously picked out on a manual typewriter by someone obviously unaccustomed to the medium. The document's somewhat ragged format, replete with spelling errors, typographical idiosyncrasies, and occasional physical distortions (resulting, I am guessing, from her pulling the sheet of paper too quickly from the platen) offer a strong visual clue to the strength and determination of this eighty-four-year-old matriarch, insistent holder of Jewish identity in our family, intent on preserving the central importance of our origins as Jews about which she had so often spoken. As such, then, a material artifact, central to this book's premise and flow.

https://doi.org/10.1515/9783110731965-013

I

I can't believe I am really doing this, but this is not a best
seller or a worst seller, it is just a kind of aotbiography,
and family history, your family history,to amuse you all— so
here it goes...
                        Oma always told me" you were a complete surprise
we were happy with our 3 children, we had a son - and then you
came along, not even a brother for Ludwig, and just when I wanted
to read the newspaper(I was born a few days after the beginning
of world war one) I wanted to name you Susanne(Figaro) but your
father confessed he still had nightmares about his childhood
nurse by that name, so we settled for Eva(Meistersinger) All
that never fazed me - it seemed just amusing to me - this optimistic
nature I inherited from my grandmother(Oma's mother) who, when
she was deported in October 1941 at the age of 84 "confessed"to
Frl. Greinert, my mother's best friend who sent her off at the
trainstation where cattlecars were used to transport the mostly
old people to Theresienstadt(Terezin)"that she could not bring
herself to use the suicide pills she was given by a friend (her
Doctor?) " because I think something good might still happen
to me"
        Being the youngest(Sophie, Maria and Ludwig were only
one to one and a half years apart from each other, I was 3 1/2
years younger than Ludwig) I was often teased, for example I was
told I was adopted, my real father was a butcher named"Krawutschke"
a very "Berlinish" name. I found that only fascinating.Our household
was typical for the bourgeois world of that time; there was a cook,
a maid and a governess. We would see our father only on Sundays,
because during the week he would come home only after we were in
bed - and I remember saying to my mother one day, during our
first family vacation after the war in the bavarian mountains
in1922, "I really like Vati very much, he is a very nice man"
My mother was flabbergasted. but then realized, I hardly ever
saw him. You, my children,remember Opa as this gentle and kind
man, which he of course was - you all know the "Struwelpeter"
(written by a Pediatrician!!!) where dreadful things happen:
The thumbsucker gets his thumbs, cut off, all that is left

of the little girl who played with matches are a pair of shoes
etc.and etc.And there is one story of the "Zappel Philip";
this boy used to move his chair back on forth, moved it toofar
back and, trying not to fall backwards grabs the tablecloth -
to no avail -he falls, pulling the tablecloth with everything
on it, down with him. There is the picture of the mother, ago-
nizing" Now the Father does not get hisndinner" This story was
to me the most frightening-one!

                                Corporal punishment was forbidden
in our house, we were never beaten.But once a governess - I was
about 3 years old, scolded me for splashing some soup on the
tablecloth on purpose, when it had been an accident, so, to
deserve the scolding I splashed some soup,this time on purpose,
and she announced she would give me a spanking - I "then I'll
laugh" She,marched us all upstairs and put me on a commode on
my stomac and started beating my behind, I laughed,the more she
beat me the more I laughed seeing the agonized but admiring
faces of my siblings, thinking" this is Triumph" It was maybe the
happiest moment of my life. The governess was gone the next day.

                                I often wondered later, as a
mother in the U.S.how much my children really were missing: there
was no maid to tease,certainly no governess to harrass,their
teachers were nuns, and they certainly would not dream of misbe=
having with their parents! poor deprived children!.

                                      For our birthdays
my father would make poems and he and my mother would recite t
them to the birthday child. And we in turn would do the same for
their birthdays,, that was a lovely tradition. When I was about
4 and Sophie about ten my mother would read all the Andersen
Fairytales to us after the midday meal, I don't know whether they
are still read bytoday's children. Somethings puzzled me at
an early age, before I was 4 years old: We all 4 said a certain
prayer each night/included the sentence" and protect all the
soldiers in the war" and I wondered " if God protected all the
soldiers the war would never end. So, even inthis happy, pro=
tected childhood there were problems I did not dare give voice to/

                                    The happiness
stopped in March 1926 - when my brother died.He was an exceptio=
nally gifted boy,academically

3

(always the first in his class, also in sports)musical, a fine
pianist and with an extraordinary gift for friendship.A wonderful
older brother. 4 years ago, I think it was in 1994 - Maria sat
next to a German Catholic Priest, ~~andxduringxinter~~ at a Carmel
Music& Festival Concert; and during intermission they started a
conversation;"What was your maiden name"he asked her - Illch -
"did you have a brother, Ludwig, at the French Gymnasium in Berlin?"
"yes!" He " Inever have forgotten this boy,he has had such an
impact on my life" - I find that extraordinary.
                                                    My childhood
ended,I was nearly 12 years old - and it was impossible for me to
ever cause my parents any worry from that time on.
                                          3 years later
I met Dad - and 4 years later I knew that we would spend the rest
of our lives together.He &nted to have 3 children, &cause he was
one of three, I wanted to have 4 because I was one of four - and
fate gave us 9 - Angela, 17 years old, said once"Each of us
siblings thinks he or she is your favorite, I know I am" And in a
certain way she is right:The one I am thinking of at that moment
is my favorite - I am sure all you parents have thissame experience.
                                          After my
brothers death Oma's oldest friend(from childhood days, sister
of Ernst Kantorowicz, the Historian, later Dad's friend) advised
her to translate French books into German, to force her to concen=
trate on something not connected with her familylife, and she did
that successfully until 1933. Among the books Maeterlinck's
"Life of the Termites," which produced not only an interesting
correspondence between the Author and Oma but also helped her
20 years later to recognize the little creatures who had invaded
the storage room for her Avon Cosmetics in our basement in Otis Street
enabling us to get rid Øf them before they had taken over the rest
of the house. After her first book appeared Opa invented this
review: ~~BadxandxIxisfixGermanyxthexeveningxxxofxourxwedding~~
          ' At last a translation that brings something different from
the original."
          My childhoodpranks were a good preparation for teenage
crimes: When my teacher Bernigau(Micky still met him when he studied
in Berlin
          in 1969) received our formal engagement announcement

4

....."to Dr.Stephan Kuttner" the name was strangely familiar to him,
then he remembered the many written notes required to be presented
after one had missed school, always signed by "Dr. Stephan Kuttner"
apparently the Family Physician,
                                Dad and I left Germany the
evening of our wedding for Italy, on the 22nd of August 1933.
Dad still had a stipend he had won half a year earlier from
some academic Institution,for a 6 months study period in Rome,so
we had some means to start out in Rome; and Dad, only 26 years
old, had a very new res^earch project all worked out --- and here
I have to talk a bit about this extraordinary combination in Dad's
life - of course Dad was uniquely talented and industrious - but
he also had extraordinary luck in his life:The then Pope, Pius Xl
before he was Pope and before he was Cardinal, was especially
interested in History of Canon law,so that, when Dad, through
the help of a Jesuit friend -was able to have his project shown
to the Pope - PiusXl understood what it was all about and decided
to finance the project through his personal means. And again-
when Dad had to leave Italy in May 1940m for Lisbon to escape
being put into a concentration Camp in Italy, an Italo-American
Professor from Catholic University in Washington appeared 2 days later
in the Vatican Library, asking for Dad. The administrator of the
Vatican Library, De Gaspery(later the first President of Italy
after world war 2) asked Monsignor Lardone why he wanted
to see Dad. That he was not there." I want to invite him as Guest
Professor to Washington,we have a new chair in the Canon Law
Faculty for the History of Canon Law,after many years of pleading
to create this chair - until now these courses were taught by
different members of our faculty, I finally succeeded" Isn't
this incredible!.   And many years later, in January 1965
in New Haven, Dad could not get rid of some kind of Flu, so
his Doctor decided to put him into Hospital for some tests,
taking routine chest Xrays they found a tumor in one lung, the
size of a PingPong ball,which was cancerous, but had nothing tO
do with the illness that brought him to the Hospital. Again,
luck was with him,and it seemed to have infected me too ---
This is a good moment in my story to tell you about the saga of
my departure from Italy. WhenDad left to go to Portugal he was

issued a Vatican Passport for himself and also for me and our
3 children. Susanne was exactly 6 weeks old.But I had been quite
ill, the trip was a long one,by train, throug h Southern Franceand
Spain, still not recovered from it's civil war and it seemed dangerous
to expose us all to uncertain hardships; Dauling Hett , who at
that time was Charge' d'Affairs in Italy, promised to get me out of
Italy in case of an emergncy "at worst, or best, as my wife No. 2 "
So we stayed. Then came this marvellous future in the U.S. All
I had to do was to get a transit Visa at the Portoguese Cosulate,
and a visa from the American Consulate. So, happily I went to the
Portughese Consulate, to be told, "show me the American Visa, and
we will give you the Transit Visa." - on to the American Consulate
to be told" show us your Portuguese Transit Visa and we will give
you the American Visa. Tableau!!! This went on for weeks,
beseeching the officials at the Portuguse place with letters from
" important people", from De Gasperi to Cardinal Mercati.. to
no avail. Practical me started selling our furniture, telling the
individual buyers : I'll put the money you give me in a special
account, - in case I do not succed(leaving you get your money
back - and in case I can leave you get what you purchased after I
will have left. - Now I have to go back a bit. In the apartment
directly under ours lived a couple exactly our age, without
children, I sometimes rode her bycicle, she sometimes borrowed
our silverware, when she had dinnerguests. So, when she came up
and was interested in buying some things, I repeated my "conditions"
of any sale. She asked" but/don't you know whether you are really
going to America?" and I told her of my problems. She then said
" Well, I can help you to get the Port.Visa" "Why can you help
me?"I went there with letters from all those important people
to no avail." She " don't you know who I am? " " Well you -
you are Pina " "Yes, but I am also the niece of so and so..
the chief of the Fascist Secret Police, the most feared man in all
of Italy! " She went on "Do you want me to take you to see
Mussolini?" (it was like somebody asking me whether I would
like to see the devil!) Pina was really like a character out of
a novel,- she told me for example she would go to very rich people and say
"I know you have, say,to pay 100.000,oo Dollars Income tax to
pay, I'll arrange it for you to have to pay only 70.000.00, you
give me 10.000.00 so you save 2o......." and did not add:or else.

6

but beeing the niece of that man everybody did what she wanted
Her uncle had no idea of all this; She also was a highly paid
Callgirl,the famous dinnerparties enhanced by my silverware
were given for her clients, among them one son of Mussolini.
On the other hand she did not want a penny from me - or from the
many jewish refugees she helped later on. A kind of Robin Hood
mentality. - I got my porfuguese Transit Visa, She brought us
to the Airprt (in the meantime, it was late in July, Italy had
entered the war travel on land was not possible any more)
my seat was taken in her name, so I had the best seat, opposite
the American Ambassador, who flew to Madrid, in this small Plane,
maybe for 20 passengers. And Susi got her first real compliment:
On hearing that we were going to immigrate to the U.S. Ambassador
Philips I think his name said:" I am proud to be the first American
to welcome such a beautiful little girl as a fellow citizen"

Arriving in Lisbon, now as EvaSarah Kuttner, witha big J
in my German Passport, we were immediately herded into a special
room - we could see inxthx Dad in the distance but were strictly
forbidden to communicate with him - we had spent the previous
night in the cellar airraid shelter, the British,on their way
to France would drop leaflets over Rome,so the children had had
maybe 3 hours of sleep and nothing to eat all since dinner the
night before (it was about 6 P.m the following day, fortunately I
was nursing Susanne.)There was not a word of complaint from t
the boys, even from my little "bad" Andrew; it seems children
instinctly know when their parents are powerless, When I complained
I was told sternly to behave myself, they were considering
to send us to Germany -1Nazi types, obviously Germans were standing
nearby - ~~has belonged for my grandmothers outside while~~
Dad had disappeared - to return about an hour later(the then
airport was close to the City) withan official of the Apostolic
Delegation and his Vatican Passport with all of us on it - we
were important people, and F R E E T O G O

Appendix II
The Outermost Edges

We engage here the voices of the remaining eight members of the third generation, arrayed along a spectrum of Jewish identity ranging from flashes of closeness to ambivalence to an unapologetic distancing. Throughout, we find echoes
of themes sounded at greater length above in Chapter 4, themes of radical Otherness, the strong gravitational pull of familial bonds, the evocative "Jewish body,"
and always, the inherited trauma of the Holocaust. We might hear these voices as
a sort of call and response to the larger narratives above. The reader is again referred to the "Family Cast of Characters" set forth in the introductory materials.

Martha:

Martha, my sister Suzanne's eldest, always felt close to her grandmother and was
fascinated by the escape stories her she recounted. As she grew older, she
learned of her great-great-grandmother's death in a concentration camp. By
then, she had developed a lively interest in her family history and in religion
in general. At college, she grew close to her roommate, an Orthodox Jew, and
heard for the first time that under Jewish law she was actually Jewish. Taking
a course in world religion, she started to "feel more Catholic" and began attending Catholic services on campus. Martha soon became close with a fellow student, Mark, a secular Jew who like herself had also been raised largely non-religiously. As they began planning their wedding, the couple decided to have both
a rabbi and a priest officiate and to have their children exposed to both Jewish
and Christian traditions. After their two children arrived, they developed a family
practice of attending High Holiday services in a synagogue and Christmas and
Easter services in a Congregational church. The children were not baptized "because Mark felt uncomfortable with it;" their son was "medically circumcised."
Their desire was to create an atmosphere in which the children would not feel
that they had to choose one or the other religion, one or the other parent, or indeed choose anything at all. To Martha, her children "seemed to feel that they
were both and that wasn't really an issue for them."

Today Martha views herself as "Judeo-Christian." She explains: "I think I feel
more Christian because during the time that I became more religious, that's really the context in which I did it. But I definitely see myself as an obvious mix."
She adds: "if Mark had felt really strongly about it and wanted me to convert,
I would've done it, I think." She sees her mother Susanne as being "mixed"

https://doi.org/10.1515/9783110731965-014

like herself, in part because, "by Jewish law, they're [the women of her family] all Jewish." When people ask, however, Martha tends to say "I was raised Christian." Because of her married surname, Fishman, she says, she is frequently invited to join Jewish organizations, to her is a reflection of Jewish snobbishness and exclusiveness. She adds, "I have definitely seen there's sort of a club of Jewish people and that's not always so welcoming if you're not Jewish." Martha finishes by affirming that for her, the "Judeo-Christian split" actually reflects continuity. "For me, it's been pretty easy to bring the two together." Paradoxically then, Martha's marriage to a Jew seems to have reinforced an inclination to assert a largely Christian identity, in part perhaps in reaction to her experience of Othering by other Jews.

Ann:

Like her siblings, Ann, Ludwig's eldest, was taught to be proud of her Jewish forebears by her (very Catholic) parents.

> [O]ur heritage, our Jewish heritage, is literally on very public view in the houses my parents have lived in. The portraits of Jakob and his wife[1], whose faces we loved. He often looked like he was disapproving, but she looked like she liked us, and was very welcoming. My parents told us that they founded a Jewish orphanage in Poznan, and that for that, they had had their portraits painted. [When asked] why is the lady wearing all that lace on her head? they said, "Ah, because they were very observant Jews, and she has her hair covered."

Today Ann sees herself as part of the "American Mix." "I say I am German Jewish, Scots, English, Irish, and on two sides, immigrant." She still identifies in many ways with her Catholic spiritual upbringing, although she is no longer affiliated. And yet, as a young scholar traveling in Germany, her first thought on getting off the train in was "They tried to kill us. But they didn't. They couldn't and I'm back." She lays claim to Berlin's Holocaust Memorial as "my family's memorial." She elaborates, "I have a big streak of being German Jewish. I've always been very public with it, in some ways, polemically so."

---

1 Her father's maternal ancestors.

Elizabeth:

Ann's younger sister Elizabeth claims both Judaism and Catholicism as part of her spiritual and cultural identity, although she practices neither. Like Ann, she learned about the family's Jewish history at home. Like Ann, she emphasizes a material heritage.

> And then we have things in the house, we have the portraits. My mother has a ring that she wears that came from my Jewish [great] great-grandmother.[2] But I was raised Catholic.

Elizabeth raised her four children with an awareness of their Jewish history and early on gave them a book of children's poetry from Theriesienstadt. Today, self-identifying as a "Seeker," Elizabeth views Judaism "as a base for Catholicism" and refers to the "Old Testament." Nonetheless she expresses a strong investment in the presence of a Jewish community around her.

> Wherever I go, I do have always a sense of, is there a Jewish community here? [I want] to see if it's healthy, and if it's safe. I just keep an eye on it. I like to see people going to service. It must be something that just feels grounding, and rounding out. Making things a little more whole.

At some point she acquired, astonishingly, a beautiful antique silver Menorah engraved with the family name, Kuttner. A friend had found it in an Arizona flea market and gave it to her. Elizabeth immediately emailed a photo of the menorah to us all.

I would say that in her inchoate way, Elizabeth expresses both alienation and longing as she embraces a communal Jewish identity at a (fearful?) remove. In her valorization of materiality as an instrument of heritage (the ring, the portraits, the Menorah), I am reminded of Hirsch's early work.[3]

John:

Johnny, Susanne's elder son, a serious student of Tibetan Buddhism, calls himself "a Jewish Buddhist." He sees Buddhism as quite compatible with what he calls an "evolved" Judaism, conceived of as "deep wisdom" or "truth," and equates Judaism with "dharma." While he tells his daughter that she has a Jewish her-

---

2 Dora Ullman.
3 See Hirsch, *Family Frames.*

itage, "if I picked one spiritual path to teach to my daughter, it would be Buddhism." Nonetheless,

> I always say I'm as Jewish as I want to be and if it's appropriate to be a Jew in that context. I used to always say I'm a Jew if someone's got a problem with Jews. I stand with my people. I feel the richness of the culture and I'm proud of being Jewish.

Johnny displays a keen and nuanced appreciation of his grandmother. "I'm just realizing now that the oral tradition of Judaism maybe is coming through a little bit in Grandma." While his relationship with his grandfather was much more limited, he nonetheless "sees him as a Jewish scholar. I have an image of scholarship and deep learning. He embodies that idea and I think of rabbi, I think of someone who's a learned person."

In sum, I would have to characterize Johnny's contact with Judaism as quite attenuated. (He cites E.L Doctorow's modernist novel *City of God* as the source of his Jewish knowledge!) Nonetheless, in a singularly sharp insight he zeros in on an inherently Jewish essence in each of his grandparents quite similar to my own, calling out both "the oral tradition" inherent in his grandmother's Jewish tales and the rabbinic quality of his grandfather's deep scholarship. Johnny expresses a great deal of pride in his Jewish origins, stressing Jewish achievements in culture and education in what is essentially a take on his German Jewish roots.

Nicholas D:

Nick relates that as a child he was told by his mother, my sister Barbara, "that we were Catholic but that we were also Jewish. And that was really confusing to me." He also remembers being told "not to tell anybody" in what he believes was an effort to protect the family interests and wellbeing. The effect on him was the "suddenly my life was a little different." He became fearful at school about antisemitic violence ("they just knew that if you were Jewish that we had to beat you up"). From this he learned "not to tell anybody [about his Jewish heritage], unless they were really a close friend." The initial story he would tell never varies: "that I was of Jewish descent, that I had some ancestors or relatives who were Jewish and that they converted to Catholicism." The rest of his story, "a broken chopped-up story," he reveals only gradually.

> I just say my grandmother and grandfather were Catholic and then as I get to know the people better and say "Well, actually they converted," [and then] I'd say, "Look, I'm Jewish." I never know if they actually understand.

As an adult, Nick has explored both Judaism and Christianity. His initial involvement with Judaism was exciting to him at first; he identified as Jewish and (rather touchingly to me) attempted to read Talmud on his own in the New York public library. He was soon daunted by what he saw as the complexity of Jewish engagement, which he saw both as "too much work" and as "exclusionary" to someone like himself, raised completely non-religiously. Indeed, he has reacted keenly to what he sees as rejection by Orthodox Jews he has known. So Nick shied away from Judaism and instead took on Christianity. "I didn't have to sit down and study one-on-one. I could just attend church on Sunday after being baptized, that was it." He briefly joined one and then another evangelical church. Today, he says,

> there's still a chance I might convert to Judaism. I think that there are a lot of beautiful things about Jewish culture and Jewish religion, the rejoiceful nature of it. Having that in your blood and in your family gives you more exposure to it.

Unlike his cousins, Nick has no recollection of having heard his grandmother's escape narratives, first learning her story from her 1998 written account. Nick's reaction to it was strong, bringing back fond memories of his grandmother, her way of speaking, her personality, leaving him wanting to know more about both his family and Judaism. "To me it was very heartwarming and certainly made me feel good" in keeping with the "joyful" and "alluring" nature of Judaism for him. Nick rejects the Holocaust as central to his Jewish identity. His reaction to *Schindler's List* is telling: "it's a big part of our history," but "whoa, you know, like what does that do for us? Does it do anything?"

In summary, Nick experienced a sort of crypto-Jewish identity, embedded early on, one in which he began experiencing himself as the secret Other. The Marrano template, peeping out! The fragmentation, the "broken-chopped-up story" of how he understands his history, has played out in his own life as he briefly joined a couple of Christian churches and still considers re-joining Judaism. His reaction to a Holocaust identity mirrors that of his cousin Abby.

Stephan P:

Stephan P., Susanne's younger son, always knew of his Jewish heritage. "My earliest memory of Mom's parents were that they were from Germany and that they were Jewish." As a teenager, he became aware "that while they didn't practice Judaism per se, it was a cultural heritage." Asked to describe his own relationship to that heritage, he describes a "familiarity" when he attends Jewish cultural events, giving as an example his friends' Jewish weddings. Indeed, among his group of close friends in college, only he and one other person were "not Jewish."

Generally, Stephan does not call himself a Jew and does not describe himself as Jewish. To him, his Jewish origins are part of a "puzzle," that includes his father's English and Irish origins. In his view, Judaism is "not just a fact of [my] history, but also a choice that one makes in terms of what one's relationship to it is." Nonetheless, while the Jewish body is never overtly mentioned in his interview,

> I started noticing about 10 years ago that when you meet peers and you're getting to know each other that somewhere between the third sentence and the tenth sentence out of someone's mouth is a little quiet mention of something related to Jewish culture. Like, maybe the word "temple" gets thrown out there, or maybe just something subtle that gives you the opportunity to say, "Oh, you're Jewish? Oh, I'm Jewish, too." I notice it all the time when I meet people, that there's this kind of quiet —like a secret handshake question.

> I like when people can't jump to conclusions about who you are. I don't mind if someone wonders if I'm Jewish or not because even though it's odd that I don't choose to actively participate in it, it's also something that passively I feel like is nothing to be ashamed of but something to be proud of.

If directly questioned, his "honest answer" is

> "My mother's side of the family were German Jews but I was not brought up Jewish at all." I don't have to worry about the fact that I don't go to synagogue if I answer the question, "Am I Jewish?" "Well, yeah, I am part Jewish." That's a fact; that's not something I get to pick and choose about.

Stephan and his wife remain resolutely non-religious and reject all forms of organized religion. They refuse to raise their two children as either Jewish or Christian.

In some ways, I would say that Stephan P. epitomizes a wholly anxiety-free, self-situating distance from Judaism. He appears to relish his chosen liminality while simultaneously displaying a comfort and quiet enjoyment in being recognized as a Member of the Tribe. While freely acknowledging his Jewish ancestry, which he qualifies as strictly cultural, and is in some sense quite proud of it, briefly citing the many achievements of Jews in modernity, he nonetheless is clear that he has no interest in further engaging with Judaism and has no interest in organized religion.

Anthony:

Like his siblings, Tony, Ludwig's youngest, learned about his Jewish heritage at the family dinner table. However, at his Catholic elementary school the nuns

> told us "Jews killed Jesus." And being aware that I had Jewish family and there was, you know, this Jewishness in me, being told that all Jews are going to hell because they killed Jesus—that sparked conversation in our family. "No, that's not how it works, that's wrong." I knew that was absolutely wrong and it was confusing. And it's a little unsettling. But it certainly contributed to my later dissatisfaction with religion, organized religion, institutions, authority, all of that. It absolutely contributed.

While he loved the family stories growing up, "stories about your parents;" especially "your mother's stories about trying to get passports and a visa—what a great story," he finds his non-Jewish mother's family story equally engaging. The Holocaust seems very "distant" to him and "a long time ago." To his children, he places

> no greater emphasis on my Jewish heritage than there is on other aspects of my heritage. My kids know that they have a Jewish heritage. They know they have a German heritage. They know they have a Polish heritage. They know they have an Irish heritage. They know they have a Catholic heritage. They know they have a Protestant heritage. They know they have all these different stories. This is where they came from.

Today Tony remains not only resolutely non-religious but also resolutely separate from his Jewish roots.

> I present myself and I think of myself in terms of the conscious choices I've made about who I am and what I'm going to be. You judge a man not by the color of his skin but the content of his character, right? And to me, my Jewish heritage is the color of my skin, not the content of my character.

Charles:

Charlie's reflections on his Jewish ancestry revolve around what he calls his "Jewish look." To illustrate, he recounts stories about people at work spontaneously wishing him Happy Hanukkah and how a rabbi once stopped him on a crosswalk to ask, "Are you Jewish?" Unlike his sisters Michele and Debbie, Charles does not regard himself as Jewish at all and forcefully rejects all bodily religious typing as inherently racist. After his father Andrew's death (he was seven), he was raised by his Swiss American Catholic mother, who emphasized his Swiss ancestry and his Swiss and Catholic family ties, and seemed unaware of any Jewishness in his father's family.

While he has many warm memories of his paternal grandmother, seeing her as the strong and loving family matriarch, and while like almost all of her grandchildren he had heard her "incredible" stories and was to eventually read her "sort of autobiography," rather astonishingly to me Charlie never has understood her narrative as Jewish at all. He now is aware of a Jewish ancestry on his father's side, but resolutely expresses no interest whatsoever in identifying with Judaism or "any religion" in any way.

Charlie marks perhaps the most distant point on the family spectrum of attitudes towards his ancestral Judaism; indeed it is only with effort that he even takes cognizance of it at all, although he is frequently brought short by largely positive reactions to his "Jewish look." To Charlie, Jews look funny, they dress funny, they eat funny. They are marked in the body as Other. The fact that he too is so marked must be difficult and confusing for him. He takes refuge in refusal, in denial it would seem.

Appendix III
Selected Family Photographs

I feature here several formal and informal photographs of my parents throughout the course of their long lives. My purpose is to foreground their dominant role in the formation of our hybrid German Jewish identity. I also include a few snapshots of the ever-expanding young refugee family of the 1940s, the last dating from approximately 1951. I finish with a group photograph of our parents with all of their (surviving) children, now adults, from our first family reunion. Dating from the late seventies, it is a shout-out to the reader, and to ourselves, of the triumphant survival of this large, quintessentially diasporic Jewish family. Without my mother's unlikely friendship with an Italian woman of dubious morality, without my father's alliances within a formal Catholic world, we would not exist.

https://doi.org/10.1515/9783110731965-015

Fig. 1: Eva and Stephan Kuttner. Civil Wedding, 1933. Kuttner Family Archives.

Fig. 2: Eva and Stephan Kuttner, Formal Wedding, 1933. Kuttner Family Archives.

Fig. 3: Eva Kuttner, 1948. Coypright Ilse Bing. Permission Granted.

Fig. 4: Stephan Kuttner, 1948. Copyright Ilse Bing. Permission Granted.

Fig. 5: Eva and Stephan Kuttner and Four Children, *circa* 1945. Kuttner Family Archives.

Fig. 6: Seven Kuttner Children, *circa* 1950. Kuttner Family Archives.

Fig. 7: Five Kuttner Children, *circa* 1946. Kuttner Family Archives.

Fig. 8: Eva Kuttner with Eight Kuttner Children, *circa* 1951. Kuttner Family Archives.

Fig. 9: Eva and Stephan Kuttner, *circa* 1985. Photograph by Elizabeth Kuttner. Permission Granted.

Fig. 10: Eva and Stephan Kuttner, *circa* 1993. Photograph by Angela Kuttner Botelho.

Fig. 11: Stephan Kuttner, *circa* 1982. Copyright Orden Pour le Mérite. Permission Granted.

Fig. 12: Eva Kuttner, 2004. Copyright RAHphoto.com. Permission Granted.

Fig. 13: Eva and Stephan Kuttner and Eight Children, *circa* 1978. Kuttner Family Archives.

Index of Persons

https://doi.org/10.1515/9783110731965-016

Printed in the USA
CPSIA information can be obtained
at www.ICGtesting.com
JSHW020456011123
51229JS00003B/120